IN MY DNA

My Career Investigating Your Worst Nightmares

LINDSEY WADE

 ONE IDEA PRESS

ISBNs

Hardcover: 978-1-944134-59-4
Paperback: 978-1-944134-70-9

For Ed and Anika

PRAISE FOR *IN MY DNA*

"Lindsey Wade in her memoir In My DNA: My Career Investigating Your Worst Nightmares exemplifies the characteristics every sexual assault and homicide investigator should have: persistence, creativity, and compassion for the victims. Lindsey's book is a must read for anybody who wants to better understand the highs and lows of being a detective, the emotional toll hearing what a sexual assault victim experienced, and the ultimate reward when all the effort culminates in finding a killer and getting a family an answer."

PAUL HOLES, Cold Case Investigator (Ret) and NY Times Bestselling author of *Unmasked: My Life Solving America's Cold Cases*

"These are the true stories of the monsters stalking our children and the dedicated detective who spent her career hunting them down. Lindsey Wade's tenacity shines through as she shares the twists and turns in solving each horrific case. From the impact the murders of two young girls had on her childhood that led to her relentless push for justice, *In My DNA* takes you inside the crime scene tape where true horrors are found."

DAVID ROSE, News Anchor, Host of *The Spotlight*

"Seldom does a writer make you, the reader, truly feel. Lindsey embodies feeling, perhaps from her DNA out. First, we feel her as a little girl, then we feel the characters in the book not only as they appear, but as they feel. We understand, almost immediately, that this Detective didn't have a job, she had emotions, duties, and feelings. She didn't have just cases, she had a real dedication to those who were victims and those who were affected by the crimes. The feelings never left her, even after years. Her ability to impart those feeling to others helped make her the success she is. Read on and you will feel too. I did, and I still do.

As the mother of Jennifer Bastian, I can speak personally to what passion, feeling and connectedness Lindsey has had with each of the cases she toiled over endlessly. For years after Jennifer's case went seemingly "cold" Lindsey was hard at work. When the public was just learning the term "cold case" Lindsey didn't care, nothing was ever "cold" to her. Her vision, her research abilities, and her doggedness influenced an entire law enforcement community. I volunteered, for a time, in her department at the Tacoma Police Department, doing research projects for Lindsey. We were both under a very strict rule that I could NEVER work on either Jenni's or Michella's cases….and I never did. Her involvement with the rape kit backlog, genetic genealogy, and advanced DNA findings brought about so much closure for so many. I am today, following the sentencing, gifted with a plea of guilty and no trial, perhaps her most appreciative fan but, way more than that, I get to call her friend."

PATTIE BASTIAN, Jennifer Bastian's Mother

"Lindsey Wade's story plays out like a Hollywood movie—complete with surprising plot twists, evil villains, and a smart, driven detective determined to solve even the most confounding crimes. *In My DNA* illustrates how a shocking experience as a child can become a calling. Lindsey Wade skillfully takes her readers on a compelling journey through the complexities of criminal justice. A page-turner from start to finish."

LINDA BYRON, Emmy Winning Investigative Reporter

"Riveting, true life story of one of the most truly dedicated, tenacious compassionate detectives in Washington State. Lindsey provides an inside look into the real everyday challenges and horrors that all detectives come face to face with: PURE EVIL!"

DAVE REICHERT, Lead Investigator on Green River Serial Murders, Retired King County Sheriff and U.S. Congressman

CONTENTS

CHAPTER 1

Bump in the Night

" Dad! Dad!—there was a man in my room!"

It's difficult to recall most memories from my early childhood, but a typical evening would have gone something like this: My dad was frying a batch of Dover Sole dipped in egg wash and Japanese breadcrumbs for my mom and me. Dad was the chef in our family, and while I liked his cooking, I hated that my hair smelled of fried fish after he made this dish. Our kitchen table was a large wooden oval shape with a removable leaf and four rolling chairs made of beige vinyl.

I rolled my chair back and forth on the linoleum as I picked at my fish—hoping my dad wouldn't notice that I hadn't finished my dinner. Since I was responsible for clearing the dinner plates, it wasn't unusual for me to covertly secrete any food I didn't want to swallow inside my Tupperware cup filled with milk. I was definitely a picky eater. After dinner, we made our way to our basement rec room to watch television.

Later that night, I sat cross-legged on my bedroom carpet, listening to my *Thriller* record on my turntable. Even though I was only about eight, I loved music—especially Michael Jackson and Prince. My dad had a big album collection, which is probably why I developed an appreciation for music at a young age. One of my favorite pastimes was taking trips to Tower Records with my Dad, where I got to pick out my own albums. I remember thinking the place was like a musical toy store, with rows and rows of magical albums covered in cellophane. On one trip, I picked out a Lionel Richie album, and on another, I selected Rick Springfield's *Working Class Dog* featuring one of my favorite songs back then—*Jessie's Girl*.

Our 1970 tri-level home had three bedrooms upstairs and a fourth in the basement. My parents' room was at the top of the stairs to the left; then, there was my room about halfway down the hall and a guest room at the far end of the hallway. On this fall evening, I had gone to sleep in my twin bed just like I always did, but then something woke me up—a bad dream?

No, I wet the bed. What happened next is burned deep into my memory. After waking my mom and telling her what happened, she helped me change into clean pajamas; then she put me to bed in the guest room at the end of the hall because we were too tired to change my sheets in the middle of the night.

The guest bedroom was chilly. It smelled old and musty—probably because we rarely used it and normally kept the door closed. There was a life-sized stuffed koala perched in the corner of the room like a sentinel, which made it a little creepy. The guest room was twice the size of mine, and the queen bed with its heavy wood frame and lattice headboard felt too big and unfamiliar to me. I crawled in between the cold sheets and tried to warm myself up by pulling the comforter up to my chin. I really wanted to be in my own bed, and I couldn't wait until morning. Despite my unease, I eventually faded off to sleep.

Through my shallow haze of sleep, I could feel someone in the room with me. I opened my eyes and tried to focus, but it was difficult. As my vision began to acclimate to the darkness, I saw a figure at the foot of the bed. At first, I thought I was dreaming, but

I quickly realized I was wide awake.

It was a man.

He was watching me. I couldn't make out his face; all I could see was a dark figure standing over me.

My heart was pounding in my chest, and I wanted to scream for my dad, but I couldn't. Despite my desperate need to flee, no sounds came out of my mouth, and I was unable to move a muscle. I was frozen.

I must have gasped because the man eventually spoke.

"I'm gonna go make some eggs," he said. Then, he turned and walked out of the room and down the hall.

Once I was sure he was gone, I sat up in bed and listened intently, waiting to hear the familiar creak of our stairs. I didn't hear anything except the thunderous sound of my own heart beating uncontrollably in my ears.

I was terrified that he would return, so after a few minutes, I worked up the courage to leave my bed. I quietly slid out from under the covers and slowly tip-toed to the door, and peered down the hall—all clear. Then, I held my breath and sprinted to my parents' bedroom at the opposite end of the hall. I jumped onto the bed and tried to shake my dad awake. "Dad, Dad! There was a man in my room!" I yell-whispered. After what felt like an eternity, my dad showed some comprehension of what I was saying, though he didn't seem overly concerned. Maybe he thought I was having a nightmare, or maybe he thought I confused the koala with a person. He finally got up and made his way downstairs to look around. I followed him to the top of the stairs and watched in horror as he went from the living room to the kitchen, then to the basement. After checking the house, my dad came back upstairs and told me there was no one in our house. I couldn't believe it.

I was absolutely petrified. I knew there had been a man at the foot of my bed just a few minutes earlier. Where had he gone?

There was absolutely no way I was going back to the guest room. I slept with my parents that night, feeling safe and secure in their bed but still afraid of what was lurking in the dark recesses of my house. Who was the scary man? Would he come back? These troubling questions bounced around in my head like pinballs until I finally dozed off—although I didn't get much sleep.

The following morning, I was still shaken. Things got worse when my dad discovered a pocket knife lying on our recliner in the basement rec room. My dad didn't recognize it, but I would find out later that he had an idea who it belonged to.

As it turned out, my parents had noticed several odd things happening at our house in the days and weeks leading up to that night. My dad normally left cash on the kitchen table for my mom before leaving for his evening shift at Boeing. On one occasion, they discovered that $20 was missing from the kitchen table. My dad also found that the screen to our basement laundry room window had gone missing.

Eventually, my dad caught the teenage boy who lived next door trying to break in one day when he thought my folks were at work. My dad was working swing shift, and my mom and I were home sick. My parents heard the doorbell ring in the middle of the day but didn't get up to answer it immediately. A few minutes later, my dad went to the front door, but there was no one there. He then walked around to the side of our house and found the neighbor boy trying to break in through the laundry room window.

According to urban legend, my dad put the fear of God into the boy, which likely included threats of serious permanent bodily injury, and he never stepped foot on our property again. My dad contacted his mother and learned that the boy had been running away and they hadn't seen him in weeks. After that, the missing window screen mysteriously made its way over our fence from the neighbor's yard. This was one of two instances in my childhood where I recall my dad laying down the law in our neighborhood.

We had moved to our house in University Place, a suburb of Tacoma, when I was six. UP is a quiet little town with a good school district. We must have raised some eyebrows when we moved in since we were the only inter-racial family in our neighborhood. My mom had been a white teenage single mother to a half-black child in the 1970s which was a challenge. I made my entrance into the world eight weeks before my due date. My mom was at a drive-in movie with friends when her water broke. I was born at Tacoma's Madigan Army Medical Center, weighing three pounds, seven ounces, and I spent the first few weeks of my life battling pneumonia in the pediatric ICU.

Since I arrived so early, Mom's baby shower happened after my birth. She told me that a friend suggested she keep the tags on all the baby clothes so that she could return them if I died. Instead, Mom promptly cut them off and washed everything. My mom was determined to bring me home from the hospital—alive.

After I was born, she struggled to make ends meet and to stay in college. My biological father, whom I would meet for the first time at age eighteen, wasn't interested in sticking around.

My mom met Jack Jackson when I was about two. They dated for a couple of years and eventually married when I was four. Jack adopted me after they were married, and I'm thankful to have such a great dad. Mom loves to tell the story about a time the three of us were riding in Dad's Oldsmobile. This was in the late 1970s, so all three of us were sitting on the car's front seat, with me in the middle. I was about three at the time, and Dad was apparently driving too fast for my liking. I turned my head to the left, glared at him, and said, "Slow down, Jackie, God-damn it!"

My dad, Jack, is half black and half Japanese. No one would have ever guessed he wasn't my biological father. In fact, my brother, sister, and I look more alike than most full siblings.

My other memory of my dad having to straighten someone out occurred a few years later after an incident at the school bus stop—which was the site of occasional hazing from neighborhood kids. One day, a white kid who routinely called me "Michael Jackson" told me that "Niggers aren't allowed at Chambers" (our elementary school). Shocked and hurt, I went home and told my dad, who had a word (or more likely many words that would have included "mother" and "fuck"), with the boy's father. That was the last time he bothered me, but it wouldn't be the last time I experienced blatant racism.

In the days following my frightening encounter with the stranger at the foot of my bed, I was jumpy and nervous about going to bed alone. My parents tried to downplay the situation, and we never really talked about what happened until many years later. Today, my dad will say that he didn't believe me when I first ran into his bedroom that night—he assumed I had a bad dream.

It's hard for me to evaluate the situation from my parents' perspective. I continually think about what I would do if my daughter barged into my room in the middle of the night with a similar message—DEFCON 1, without a doubt. In their defense, I base that on my training and experience as a police officer and as a sex crimes detective, not an average citizen who isn't completely jaded and who doesn't think everyone and their brother is a sex offender.

Looking back on the terrifying experience of finding a stranger at the foot of my bed—and knowing what I know now about sexual predators—I'm lucky he only wanted breakfast. That said, I do wonder how many other times he secretly crept around inside our house in the middle of the night undetected.

CHAPTER 2

Girls in the Park

" *Up until that point, I didn't know that evil existed or that monsters were real.*"

I loved riding my shiny red ten-speed Schwinn around my neighborhood in the summer of 1986. An eleven-year-old tomboy through and through, I was sometimes mistaken for a boy thanks to my close-cropped curls. In third grade, I asked my dad to teach me how to play softball. He was thrilled and insisted on teaching me how to play softball *the right way*. My lessons included the mantra, "Don't throw like a girl." By the time I began playing in a league, my teammates were afraid to pitch to me or even play catch because—according to my dad—"She definitely did not throw or hit like a girl." I think I *did* throw and hit like a girl; he just wasn't aware of the power girls could have. He quickly learned.

When I wasn't splashing around in the plastic wading pool in our front yard with my baby brother, I was pushing him around the house in a laundry basket that doubled as a mini race car. The hit song *Kiss* topped the Billboard charts that April, and my love for Prince was evident—thanks to a huge Purple Rain poster that hung in my room. By August, Madonna's "Papa Don't Preach" was burned into my brain thanks to continuous airplay on MTV.

On any given night, My dad and I were in the driveway

shooting hoops during that warm month of August. He really wanted me to play basketball on a team, but I had no interest. Neighborhood boys whizzed by on their skateboards, and some nights they stopped to say, "Hi," or join in the game. It was during this carefree time in my childhood that I heard about the little girls who'd been killed while playing in north Tacoma parks. One of the girls, 12-year-old Michella Welch, was last seen alive by her sisters at Puget Park on March 26th, 1986. Roughly four months later, 13-year-old Jennifer Bastian went missing while out for a bike ride at Point Defiance Park and was found dead a few weeks later.

I can't recall the exact moment when I heard about these horrifying disappearances and deaths. Thinking back on it now, it was just something everyone knew about. Point Defiance was the very same park where I'd spent so many wonderful summer days in the YMCA day camp combing the beach for seashells, turning over rocks in search of bright orange baby crabs, playing games in the woods, and making arts and crafts projects out of yarn and sticks collected from the park.

On the afternoon of August 4, 1986, thirteen-year-old Jennifer Bastian left her house for a bike ride in Point Defiance Park. The park was located in the 5400 block of North Pearl Street in Tacoma. Point Defiance Park is one of the largest parks in Washington State, surrounded by the Puget Sound and encompassing 760 acres, including a zoo, beach, and densely forested trails surrounding a paved road called the Five Mile Drive. Five Mile Drive is a popular area for runners and cyclists, consisting of a one-lane road surrounded by densely wooded trails on both sides. All traffic is forced to move in a single direction with turnouts that open into viewpoints overlooking the water. The trails allow cyclists, runners, and hikers to move off the roadway and also provide shortcuts between viewpoints.

Jennifer Bastian would have been an eighth-grader at Truman

Middle School the following month. She left her house that balmy August afternoon on her shiny new 18-speed Schwinn to train for an upcoming ride in the San Juan Islands. Known as Jenni by family and friends, the blonde, blue-eyed teen wore a pixie haircut fashionable at the time. Jennifer was petite for her age, but that never held her back—she was a strong athlete and took her training seriously.

The Bastian residence was located in the 2100 block of North Winnifred, which was approximately three miles from the entrance to the park. She lived there with her parents, Ralph and Pattie, and her older sister, Theresa. Ralph owned a travel agency, and Pattie worked in sales for AT&T. Fifteen-year-old Theresa worked as a YMCA day camp counselor that summer at Point Defiance. She was working in the park on August 4.

Before leaving the house that afternoon, Jennifer got permission to go to the park alone. Normally she rode with a buddy, but her riding partner wasn't available that day. After penning a note for her parents saying she would be back by 6:30 PM, Jennifer set out for the picturesque park at about 2:30 in the afternoon.

She never came home.

6:30 came and went—no sign of Jennifer. After Ralph and some of the neighbors searched the neighborhood, including her normal route to and from the park, Jennifer's mother raced home from work. The Bastians called Tacoma Police to report Jennifer missing at 8:30 PM. Ralph and Pattie told Officer Dave Wiltfong their daughter was an avid cyclist who rode to the park several times a week to train.

The report of a missing teenage girl from a north-end park was too ominous to ignore, since four months earlier, twelve-year-old Michella Welch was abducted and murdered in another park located in the north end of Tacoma, just three miles away. Her killer was still on the loose. Had he struck again?

At 1:00 AM, Officer Wiltfong contacted Northwest Bloodhounds and requested their assistance. Two dog handlers responded with their bloodhounds and obtained a couple of Jennifer's personal belongings from Pattie to use as scent articles. The dogs tracked Jennifer's scent from her home to the park and by 5:30 AM, the dogs completed their track. They picked up her scent on the Five Mile Drive—but they didn't find her.

The Five Mile Drive of Point Defiance Park was closed to the public August 5th-7th while police conducted a massive search which involved approximately two hundred thirty searchers each day. The Bastian family and their friends handed out missing person posters at the park entrance, and Pattie's employer—AT&T—provided four primitive brick-style cell phones to the command center for use during the search. Search and Rescue volunteers from all over the state combed the trails under a canopy of towering evergreens while searchers on ATVs and horseback traversed acres of thick underbrush. After the three-day search by hundreds of volunteers, there was still no sign of Jennifer. There were several reported sightings on the day she went missing, including the following reports:

Between 2:30 and 3:00 PM — A park employee called Jennifer's parents and advised them he had seen Jennifer riding her bike near the Owen Beach entrance.

Around 4:10 PM — Three boys who knew Jennifer reported they passed her going the opposite direction on Five Mile Drive. They said a white male adult riding a racing type Huffy ten-speed and wearing mirrored sunglasses was riding close behind her. When she sped up or slowed down, the man did the same. A sketch of this man was developed as a possible suspect, but he was never identified.

At 4:20 PM — A woman reported seeing a young white female believed to be Jennifer, pulling into the second viewpoint past Owen Beach. She described the girl as wearing a blue or purple swimsuit, shorts, and a bicycle helmet. This clothing description is consistent with what Jennifer was wearing.

A day camp counselor reported seeing a girl matching Jennifer's description at Owen Beach around 3:15, then again later between 4:00 and 4:40, riding her bike in front of the lodge inside the park.

Between 3:00 and 5:00 PM — Two young men reported they were drinking beer at the Dalco Passage Viewpoint when a girl matching Jennifer's description rode up and had a conversation with them. They said she had taken her helmet off, and it fell on the ground. She drank from a water bottle and told them she was training for an upcoming bike ride. One of the men recalled that she was wearing either two silver bracelets or a necklace looped twice around her wrist. Jennifer was, in fact, wearing three sterling silver bracelets that day. They were a gift from her dad—souvenirs from a trip to Mexico. Jennifer and her mother always wore silver bracelets. Pattie Bastian still wears hers every day.

5:30 PM — A man reported seeing a girl consistent with Jennifer's description approaching the park entrance from the Five Mile Drive. He said he noticed her because she looked so young and had such professional-looking bike equipment.

At about 5:45 PM — Another man reported seeing a young white female on a bicycle on the Five Mile Drive near the zoo. His description of her appearance and clothing was consistent with Jennifer.

Around 6:00 PM — A woman reported seeing a girl fitting Jennifer's description in the bowl area of the park. Her clothing description was consistent with Jennifer's.

All of these sightings confirmed Jennifer had made it to the park and had ridden her bike along the Five Mile Drive—but none of this information helped police find her.

Days turned into weeks. Psychics called in with visions of where Jennifer was located, dozens of citizen tips were followed up, but nothing concrete came of them. Early on, there was speculation that Jennifer had been abducted by someone in a black van and had been taken out of the park. This was based on information from a man who reported he was walking with his daughter on Five Mile Drive between 2:00 and 2:30 PM and witnessed a young girl matching Jennifer's description, riding a bike, being forced into a black van. The man reported hearing a male inside the van say, "Didn't I tell you to get into the van?" Then the girl and her bike were shoved into the van by a white male on a bike. This info was disseminated to the media, and dozens of tips were called in regarding suspicious black vans. The van was later ruled out as being related based on numerous credible sightings of Jennifer in the park after this allegedly occurred.

At 8:00 PM on August 26, a man called the park police to report that he was jogging with the YMCA running club on a trail near the Five Mile Drive and noticed a foul odor. Park police, along with Tacoma Police Officers, arrived and attempted to locate the source of the odor with no success. A police K9 was called in but still could not locate the source of the odor.

At 2:00 PM on August 28, A German Shepherd Search Dog made a discovery in a wooded area off Five Mile Drive between the road and the cliffs, south of the Gig Harbor Viewpoint, about one hundred and fifty feet off the main path. The location was well hidden and difficult to access. The body of a young female was found inside a cave-like hollowed-out area within the brush and trees, obscured from view from the nearby trail.

Twenty-four days after she went missing, Jennifer was finally located.

According to Dr. Mark Papworth, Thurston County Deputy Coroner called to the scene, the hiding spot looked like it had been prepared ahead of time. He also wrote in his report that he believed the crime was carefully organized and that it had been practiced in fantasy or with a previous victim.

Jennifer's bike was located southwest of her body toward the cliff, lying in the brush, just south of the path. The bike was covered with fern fronds that had dried up and turned brown. Members of the Green River Task Force had become skilled at outdoor homicide investigation, so they were called in to assist Tacoma Police detectives with processing the crime scene.

At the time of her discovery, Jennifer was found lying on her back. Her swimsuit and shorts had been pulled down around her right ankle. It appeared Jennifer had been posed and based on the positioning of her body; it appeared she had been sexually assaulted. Her bicycle helmet was found in her saddlebag, but she was still wearing her socks, tennis shoes, and riding gloves.

At her autopsy, Jennifer was described as a white female, thirteen years old, 4'8" and estimated to weigh 70-75 pounds, with short blonde hair. Very little was able to be determined during the postmortem exam due to decomposition, but a thin ligature was found looped around Jennifer's neck. The Medical Examiner ruled the cause of death asphyxia secondary to ligature strangulation and concluded the appearance of Jennifer's clothing indicated sexual assault.

When the news of the discovery broke, Tacoma was in a panic. In the span of five months, not one but two young girls had been found brutally murdered in North Tacoma parks. Just a few months before Jennifer disappeared, 12-year-old Michella Welch was found raped and murdered in a wooded gulch adjacent to a small neighborhood park not far from Point Defiance. Both girls were blue-eyed blondes who'd been out riding their bikes when they went missing. Michella's murder was still unsolved. Was there a serial killer on the loose? This was a turning point in the city. Parents began keeping their children indoors; kids weren't allowed to play outside alone. The parks weren't safe anymore. The innocence of many was shattered thanks to these tragedies.

I didn't know Jennifer or Michella, but that didn't matter. The idea that something so unbelievable could happen to a young girl out riding her bike was terrifying to me. My friends heard about what happened too. We were scared to ride our bikes and scared to walk alone, afraid it could happen to us. Grown-ups also took notice, and the days of free-range parenting became a thing of the past in Tacoma. The senseless slayings changed the way parents raised their kids and the way kids looked at the world.

Up until that point, I didn't know that evil existed or that monsters were real.

The stories were all over the newspapers and on TV. What if the killer was still out there? Would he do it again?

Before the killings, I was a carefree kid—oblivious to the dangers lurking beyond my safe middle-class suburban neighborhood. After learning that two girls had been murdered while they were out doing the same kinds of things I liked to do—riding their bikes—I was scared. Playing in the woods now gave me the creeps.

A couple of years later, in junior high, I occasionally walked to school by myself when I missed the bus or couldn't get a ride. My route required me to walk past a wooded gulch which always made the hair on the back of my neck stand up. As I approached, my heart would race, and I would cross the street in order to put some distance between me and the tree line, then walk as fast as I could to get past it. Even though it seemed ridiculous, I always pictured some deranged lunatic hiding in the trees, waiting to grab me as I walked past. That constant fear was embedded in me at an early age, from the time the man was at the end of my bed to learning about Jennifer and Michella being found murdered.

It's hard for me to think back to a time in my childhood when the mystery surrounding Michella and Jennifer wasn't in the backdrop. It was just something that everyone knew about—a town tragedy that shaped our childhood. My mom likened it to her teenage years when the "Ted" killer was on the loose. She couldn't tell me when she first heard about the missing young women, but she had been warned about "Ted" just as every other young female with long hair parted in the middle had been. Ted Bundy became an urban legend, cemented into the minds of generations of Washingtonians.

There was no question that the unsolved murders of Jennifer and Michella had a devastating impact on Tacoma and the surrounding communities—many of the people affected had no personal connection to the victims or their families. The outrageous murders were etched into the landscape of our town—and into the psyches of many young girls—including me.

The baffling mystery hung like a dark cloud over Tacoma, leaving an indelible mark that wouldn't be erased for three decades.

CHAPTER 3

My First Taste

" *After absorbing every detail of the book, I knew I wanted to be a detective just like Bob Keppel."*

I was a sophomore in high school when I came upon a book at the library about Ted Bundy called *The Stranger Beside Me* by Ann Rule. As I devoured each page of the book, I became mesmerized by the story—and horrified at the same time. I was also fascinated with how the investigation unfolded. I imagined what it must have been like for the detectives—especially the lead detective—Bob Keppel—to juggle so many cases with almost nothing to work with. I visualized what the wild, rugged terrain must have been like at Taylor Mountain, where several sets of skeletal remains of young women were found. I wondered how the police were able to comb through thousands of tips about "Ted" and figure out which ones were viable and which ones were useless. It seemed like the investigators were trying to put together a jigsaw puzzle made up of thousands of random pieces—only they didn't have the box to see what it was supposed to look like in the end. I was hooked.

For those not familiar with Ted, a quick recap: Ted Bundy is one of the most notorious serial killers in U.S. history. His reign of terror began in the Seattle area during the early 1970s. According to a timeline created by the FBI, Bundy confessed to murdering thirty young women and girls between 1974 and 1978 in seven states: Washington, Oregon, California, Colorado, Utah, Idaho, and Florida. His first confirmed victim, Lynda Healy, was a twenty-one-year-old University of Washington student who lived near the campus. During the early morning hours of February 1, 1974, Bundy crept into Healy's basement bedroom and abducted her from her bed without alerting her sleeping roommates. Bundy is suspected of killing many more women and girls, but he took most of his secrets to the grave when he was executed in Florida's electric chair on January 24, 1989, for the abduction and murder of twelve-year-old Kimberly Leach.

I couldn't believe the series of unbelievable events described in vivid detail within the book were true—and they happened very near where I lived in Washington. I was intrigued that, like me, Bundy grew up in Tacoma. Another eerie coincidence was the fact that my mom knew his mother from the office at the University of Puget Sound, a small private college in Tacoma.

The Tacoma connection was fascinating —but what was even more captivating to me was the feeling of absolute terror I experienced thinking about what his innocent victims must have endured. I pictured myself in many of the same scenarios his victims found themselves in—after all, girls are taught to be polite and accommodating. Being rude or blunt would be a display of bad manners. Historically, women have ignored their instincts, alerting them to danger because they don't want to overreact or, God forbid—offend someone. Offering to help a stranger in need or walking to my car alone after dark were things I would have done, and the idea that a chameleon-like predator named Ted Bundy could be out there waiting to pounce was absolutely appalling to me. I identified with his victims—and I knew I didn't want to end up like them.

Reading about the shocking details of Bundy's crimes brought me right back to the feeling of dread I experienced when I woke to find a stranger at my own bedside years earlier. I also thought about Jennifer Bastian, and I wondered if the person responsible for her death was the same kind of monster as Ted Bundy. After absorbing every detail of the book, I knew I wanted to be a detective just like Bob Keppel. I wanted to catch men like Ted Bundy, and Ann Rule's book inspired the course for my life to come.

After graduating from Curtis High School in 1994, I went off to college at Western Washington University. After a semester, I decided Western wasn't for me, so I moved back to Tacoma and enrolled at Tacoma Community College (TCC). Two important things happened at TCC.

First, I met Tacoma Police Sergeant Barbara Justice in one of my classes, and she agreed to allow me to do an internship with her. Barb was an amazing woman who entered into the field of law enforcement in 1977 when females were not widely accepted. Barb had sparkling blue eyes and straight dark brown hair that she usually pulled into a simple ponytail at the base of her neck. She was friendly and willing to share her experiences and knowledge with me. It turned out that her daughter and I had the same birthday and graduated in the same class at Curtis High School, which was a surprising coincidence.

The internship was pretty informal, but by this time, I knew I wanted to be a police officer and eventually a detective, and who better to give me a glimpse into the mysterious world of police work than a veteran female cop? I got to tag along with Barb during her shift after class several times a week, and she even took me to the range to shoot—that was a blast, especially since I got to shoot a real police pistol, which would end up being the same kind of pistol I would be issued as a new recruit. The gun was massive and heavy—a .40 caliber Beretta 96-D which was kind of a pain to shoot because it was double action only, so it took a significant amount of pressure to pull the trigger. Despite the gun, I was a naturally good shot and had been to the range with my dad many times.

At the time of my internship with Barb, she was the Drug Abuse Resistance Education (DARE) Sergeant, and her unit worked out of a substation at the Tacoma Mall. I got to meet quite a few officers and see some of the inner workings of the department first-hand.

One of the officers I met was a female motorcycle cop, which was something I'd never seen before. Her appearance surprised and impressed me. She was tall—close to six feet, I think, and when she removed her helmet, I could see she had short blonde hair that somehow looked feminine despite its length. She wore a stylish cream-colored scarf over her rugged black leather jacket and black leather knee-high motorcycle boots. Damn, this woman looked impressive. She definitely had *Police Presence*—her bearing and appearance commanded respect.

During the three months of my internship with Barb, she became a friend and mentor to me, showing me around the city and pointing out things only cops notice. As an example, one day, we were stopped at a red light in her burgundy unmarked Pontiac Grand Prix. She noticed a man looking hard at her car and said, "He knows we're the POLICE." I was perplexed—how could he tell, I wondered. She told me it was the small silver antennae on the trunk and the exempt license plate. Up to this point in my life, I had never noticed either of these things on vehicles.

Barb became a trusted ally and someone I continued to look to for advice as my career took off.

The second important thing that happened was that I took a class at TCC from Sam Holden, a Police Detective, and the hiring officer for the Tacoma Police Department.

I adored Sam from the start, in a fatherly sort of way. He had a slow southern accent and kind eyes. I loved hearing the stories he told about police work and his techniques for interviewing suspects. During one of our lectures, Sam talked about how he could get child molesters to talk to him. He would reinforce a suspect's mental distortions by saying something like, "I bet she looked pretty sexy in those Garfield underwear" or "I know she was probably flirting with you." Now we're talking about a guy who molested a five-year-old, but in the suspect's twisted mind, it really happened that way. I remember being skeptical that anyone would really confess using such tactics, but years later, when I began working as a detective in the Special Assault Unit, I found out just how well these techniques work.

Sam brought several Tacoma Police Officers into class as guest speakers. One traffic officer used the term DWHUA to describe one motorist's bad driving—Driving With Head Up Ass. That was pretty funny. Sam set me up on a couple of ride-alongs on swing shift in Tacoma, and I was hooked. There was no doubt in my mind that I wanted to be a Tacoma Police Officer.

I enrolled in TCC's reserve police academy. The reserve academy was set up at the college and mainly consisted of classroom lectures. Outside the classroom, we practiced defensive tactics and got to drive fast in police cars on an Emergency Vehicle Operations Course. I had no intention of becoming a reserve officer, but the training was good preparation for the full-time basic law enforcement academy I would have to complete if I wanted to make police work a career.

Tacoma is a port city situated along the shores of Puget Sound, about thirty miles south of Seattle. The population is just over 200,000, and the city features beautiful beaches and parks along with a waterfront promenade called Ruston Way.

Despite its beauty, there are some rough neighborhoods— Tacoma has battled more than its fair share of drugs and gangs. Over the years, many have puzzled about why we have such a sordid history of violent crime in the Pacific Northwest, especially our track record of breeding homegrown serial killers like Gary Ridgeway, Ted Bundy, and Robert Yates—just to name a few. Some blame the depressingly overcast weather that settles into the area in late fall and doesn't usually let up until the end of spring—perhaps leading to seasonal affective disorder or Vitamin D deficiency-induced psychosis.

Despite what you've probably seen on TV, the sun does actually shine in Western Washington, and the gorgeous summers here are unrivaled. I bought a tee-shirt that sums up my hometown perfectly: *Tacoma - a little bit ghetto, whole lot of wonderful.* It's not too big, not too small, and not too bougie.

CHAPTER 4

Night Patrol

" *Oh shit... he's trying to kill me."*

After earning my associate degree from Tacoma Community College, I enrolled at the Steilacoom satellite branch of Central Washington University. I applied with the Tacoma Police Department, and after scoring well on the written test, I began the lengthy hiring process, which included an oral board, physical agility test, medical exam, psychological exam, polygraph, and background investigation. During my oral board, I was asked by one of the male officers on the panel if I'd ever been in a fight. I could tell he was skeptical that I could handle myself on the mean streets of Tacoma. I answered, "Yes."

The panel members looked surprised and asked for more details. I explained that I had been involved in a bar fight in Mexico on my senior trip. They laughed, but looking back on it now, I'm pretty sure they wouldn't have asked a male candidate that question. Also, I doubt they could get away with asking something like that today.

After my first quarter at Central, I was offered my dream job by Detective Sam Holden, so I quit school to join the Tacoma Police Department on March 31st, 1997. I was determined to finish college, so I eventually returned to school and took night classes. I earned my bachelor's degree in law and Justice with a minor in Psychology in 2006 from Central Washington University.

When I was hired by the Tacoma Police Department, I'd been dating a guy who also wanted to become a police officer. Though I'd hoped he would have been happy for me when I got hired for my dream job, he really wasn't. He was controlling, jealous, and manipulative. He tried to discourage me by saying things like, "Your field training officers are going to want to have sex with you."

On the night before my first day of work at the Tacoma Police Department, he left a revolting hickey on my neck. I didn't notice it until the following morning as I dressed for my first big day. I was livid—what a childish thing to do. He was acting like a dog marking his territory. I was able to conceal the mark by wearing a turtleneck that day, but needless to say, the relationship didn't last long after that, and I dumped him while I was in the academy.

After graduating from the police academy as one of six women—and the only woman of color in our class of twenty-nine recruits, I spent my first five years as a police officer working the graveyard shift on patrol in Tacoma's Hilltop neighborhood, often referred to as "The Hill." I was a fresh-faced twenty-two-year-old who probably looked more like a girl than a woman. I weighed about a hundred and twenty pounds soaking wet and wore a short ponytail at the base of my neck. It wasn't uncommon for someone to mistake me for one of the high school-aged Police Explorers. My gear—including the ballistic vest, duty belt, handgun, extra magazines, baton, two sets of handcuffs, flashlight, and radio equaled close to a quarter of my body weight. The molded plastic holster for my gun dug into my hip night after night, causing me to be continually sore and bruised.

I quickly realized this was a common problem for female officers because we have hips, and men don't. After testing out several methods to ease the pressure on my hip from the gun belt and holster—including adhesive pads and kitchen sponges, I finally found a sound long-term solution—youth football pads. I purchased a set of hip pads at a local sporting goods store, and each night before my shift, I tucked them into my bike shorts. They were a Godsend. I passed my trick along to some of my fellow female officers who'd also been in search of relief from the gun belt.

During my second month on the street, my field training officer and I responded to an overdose at the Travel Inn, a drug-infested shithole motel on Pacific Ave, known for drugs and prostitution. Inside the grungy room, we found an unconscious man lying on his back on the filthy brown carpet. Body odor and cigarette smoke hung thick in the air. Another man, presumably his friend, was giving mouth to mouth. When he saw us, the good Samaritan sat up, chunks of vomit dangling from his matted beard as he yelled for help. One of the senior officers on the scene—a grizzled dayshift dinosaur, told the man in his cool, calm voice, "Keep on blowing; you're doing good."

I went to my first dead body call during my third month of field training. The victim died while sitting on her couch and appeared to have been dead for several days. Her body was severely bloated, and although she was white, her skin had turned deep shades of purple and black. The unmistakable thick greasy stench was overwhelming. I was thankful the Fire Department made me wear a respirator while I was inside the house, especially when we moved the body and she split open. At that point, the stench was practically three-dimensional. As luck would have it, I had borrowed a long-sleeve wool uniform shirt from another officer that shift, and I don't think the odor of putrefaction was ever fully eradicated from the garment. From that day forward, I couldn't handle the smell of fast-food fried chicken—which in my mind, smelled exactly like that rotting corpse.

I had a few partners while I was on patrol, and we had a lot of fun in those days. For someone who's never experienced it, it's hard to articulate the deep bond forged between partners in police work. Aside from the fact that I spent more time with my partners than my own family, I also trusted them completely. I knew they would have laid down their lives for me, and I would have done the same for them.

My first partner didn't take kindly to anyone disrespecting me. As an example, a drunk we arrested one night kept calling me Daisy Mae instead of Officer Jackson. Big mistake. He eventually realized it was best to just shut up after the tongue-lashing he received.

The Hill was pretty busy in those days, but nothing like what it had been in the late 80s and early 90s. Several batches of Los Angeles gang members moved up to Tacoma and staked a claim. According to a Tacoma gang expert, the Inglewood Family Bloods were the first gang set to move into Tacoma's Hilltop neighborhood. They were eventually forced over to the east side by a combination of the Los Angeles Crips—including the Watergate and Rollin 60s Crips—and pressure from the cops. Soon a group of young locals formed their own set called the Hilltop Crips, which is still operational today. In those early days, drive-by shootings and open-air drug dealing became the norm. The rivalry between the gangs—fueled by the sale of crack cocaine—wreaked havoc on Tacoma.

By 1997, things had slowed down considerably, but the open-air drug-dealing and gang violence were still present. An average Saturday night might consist of a few domestic dispute calls, drug activity complaints, a fight or two, maybe a shooting or stabbing.

One night, my partner and I responded to a domestic dispute at South 9th & M Street, also in the Hilltop neighborhood. A man had beaten his girlfriend and then jumped through a window and then managed to climb onto the roof of the house. Another officer and I cornered the suspect on the front porch of a nearby residence. It was pitch black outside, and despite our repeated commands to show his hands, the suspect kept them firmly planted inside his coat pockets. We had him at gunpoint, and I was yelling so loud there was no need to give our location over the radio. My partner could hear me from his position clearly at the other end of the block.

After a few more seconds, the suspect pulled his hands from his pockets, revealing the object in his hand—a hairbrush. I was furious. That was the closest I ever came to shooting a suspect. We had no idea what he had in his hand but based on the violence he'd inflicted on his girlfriend and his furtive actions; we assumed he had a weapon. Thank God I didn't shoot him. Having to explain shooting a man armed with a hairbrush would have been a nightmare because the public and media don't really understand the split-second decision-making required in a situation like that. As a police officer, hesitating for even a moment could be the difference between living and dying. If the man had been armed with a gun, waiting until he pulled it out and pointed it at me would have been too late. Luckily that wasn't the case.

One night on patrol, my partner and I responded to a back-up call from another officer in a foot chase. When we arrived, we found that the suspect had run into the home of an unknown citizen and was trying to hide under a bed. The officer was trying to pull him out while holding the bed up with her other arm—Wonder Woman style. Once we dragged him out from under the bed, I straddled the guy's back as I tried to pull his arms behind him. My partner got the cuffs on, but we quickly discovered that he had somehow managed to handcuff the guy's arms around my legs. Thankfully, I was young and limber and had no trouble shimmying my way out of the awkward predicament. The whole scene was like a seriously fucked up game of twister, and my partner and

I laughed about it for a long time after that.

On another night, we were searching a car downtown when I pricked my finger with a dirty hypodermic needle. The standard protocol after a needlestick was a heavy-duty regimen of drugs known as the AIDS cocktail. The atrocious smorgasbord of medications made me violently ill. The experience was extremely unpleasant, but it taught me a valuable lesson about using caution when searching people and vehicles—look before you touch, dummy.

My most memorable night on patrol would be the time a suspect tried to kill me.

My partner and I had just walked out of the Hilltop substation when we heard yelling from a house across the street. We called out on the radio that there was a possible domestic dispute and then walked over to investigate. There were several uncooperative people inside the house, and we attempted to separate the involved parties to find out what happened. My partner and I were walking the male half of the problem outside when he began to fight with us. We tried to handcuff him, but he tensed up and kept pulling away. My partner tried to stabilize him against the trunk of a car, but each time we tried to bend him forward, he popped back up like a jack-in-the-box. This guy was wiry and very strong, and we couldn't get his hands behind his back.

I remember the blank look on his face—what's known as the "thousand-yard stare." At some point during our unsuccessful attempts to get him handcuffed, I realized he was trying to pull my gun out of my holster. Oh shit… he's trying to kill me.

During the fight, we bounced off the hood of a car and then somehow ended up on the ground. I hit the pavement, and I can still remember the squeaking sound I made after having the wind knocked out of me. The bad guy landed on top of me, and my partner was on top of him.

I was on my back looking into this guy's eyes, but there was no expression. Blank. I plastered one of my hands across the top of my holster to ensure my gun stayed there. With my free hand, I grabbed the guy by the balls and tried to turn them into something resembling balloon animals. No response.

What the fuck was this guy on?

At the same time, my partner had one cuff on and wasn't letting go. After what seemed like an eternity (probably only a few seconds), the other officers on the porch who'd arrived saw what was happening on the street and came to assist. Then the miscreants from the problem house poured out into the street, including the bad guy's wife or girlfriend, who tried to jump in the fray. Once the bad guy was finally handcuffed, I could breathe again.

That was one of the scariest nights of my life. I have no doubt the guy would have shot me and probably my partner if he had been successful in his attempt to take my gun. Thankfully, he wasn't.

The five years I spent on patrol were filled with experiences that taught me valuable lessons while creating lifelong friendships. Each shift was something different, and I never knew what to expect. That said, I knew I wanted to do more. My husband Ed, who was also in law enforcement, considered himself a meat and potatoes kind of officer—control the situation, stop the bleeding, keep order, move on. I was the opposite—I got fixated on the minutia. I wanted to know everything. Give me all the juicy details, and don't leave anything out. I wanted to work a case from beginning to end. I wanted to uncover the fine details and the hidden clues in an investigation. I wanted to serve search warrants, interrogate suspects and put all the puzzle pieces together. I didn't want to just take reports in the field and then hand them off to be followed-up on. I wanted to solve cases. I wanted to be a detective.

CHAPTER 5

David 435

" *I knew I would never be able to forget what I had seen in those pictures—the images were permanently burned into my brain.*"

After patrolling the Hilltop neighborhood for five years, I took the detective test, which consisted of a written exam and an oral board. In order to be promoted to detective, officers are required to test and then be placed on an eligibility list which is good for two years.

Study materials—including state laws, criminal procedures, and departmental regulations, were posted prior to the written test. I was serious about becoming a detective and even took flashcards with me on my honeymoon. Instead of perusing *Us Weekly* or a romantic beach read on our Caribbean cruise, there I was, lying next to the pool with a margarita in one hand and my flashcards in the other. After taking the written exam and passing the oral board, I was placed on an eligibility list where I waited for just over a year to get promoted to detective. During that year on the waiting list, I transferred to Narcotics, where I learned how to write and serve search warrants, conduct surveillance, and investigate drug-related crimes. This was a good training ground for becoming a detective.

In August 2003, I was called to Chief Don Ramsdell's office, where he told me he was promoting me to detective. Had I known I was going to be promoted that day, I would have made a different outfit choice—I was dressed in shorts and a tee-shirt. Nevertheless, I was issued a shiny new detective badge with my ID number "435" inscribed on the shield, and I was assigned a new call sign, too—David 435 (all detective call signs began with the designator "David"). I was thrilled but also a little surprised because I had been chosen ahead of another candidate who was ranked ahead of me on the list.

Years later, I heard there were officers that were unhappy with me being promoted ahead of the white male officer ranked one position ahead of me on the list. One comment relayed back to me was that I had only been promoted because I was a minority female. It reminded me of another sore spot from my teenage years. A white boy I had been dating in high school told me that his mother saw my school picture and asked what race I was. When he told her I was mixed—black and white—she ordered him to stop seeing me. We didn't stop dating, but let's just say I was never invited over for Sunday dinner. The realization that someone would dislike me or believe I wasn't good enough based solely on the color of my skin was a painful reality check. And here it was coming up again in my professional life. While I knew my work spoke for itself, it still pissed me off that someone I worked with would make that accusation.

I was originally assigned to do background investigations on new hire applicants; then, I was assigned to auto theft for a few months. When the Special Assault Unit Sergeant asked me if I was interested in working for him in sex crimes, I jumped at the opportunity.

My first case in sex crimes was a walk-in at the station, which was a little unusual. In my experience, most victims call the police or go to the hospital to report a sexual assault, but sometimes they do come into the station. The woman came in to report that she was raped by an unknown man the previous evening at a house somewhere in the Hilltop neighborhood. I interviewed the woman and then sent her to the hospital for a sexual assault examination. I worked on the case for months, but I was unable to identify the suspect. The crime lab got a DNA profile from her clothing, and it was entered into the DNA database with no match. That case would remain unsolved for twelve years. The suspect's DNA was finally collected at the time of an unrelated arrest in Alaska, and it matched the unknown suspect DNA profile from my case in 2004.

The first child abuse case I was assigned was a Child Protective Services referral made by a therapist who'd reported a client disclosing information about sexual abuse that had occurred years earlier when she was a child. My sergeant thought it would be a simple case for me. It involved a convoluted assortment of multi-generational, interfamilial child molestation allegations and ritualistic child abuse. Easy case, right? Not so much. After spending several months investigating, there was not enough evidence to charge anyone. Welcome to sex crimes.

I quickly learned that adult and child sex crimes were some of the most difficult cases to investigate and prosecute. There's often no physical evidence and usually no witnesses to the crime. With that being said, I believed in the important work I was doing, and I was committed to seeking justice for victims. To me, being a detective was more than a job—it was a calling. It wasn't nine to five with weekends off. Aside from the long hours followed by midnight callouts that often claimed the whole weekend, my cases were always on my mind. Whether I was at home or at work, I was always replaying, planning, and analyzing my investigations in my head. Some cases were more involved than others.

After a few months into working sex crimes, one of the "old

guys" in Homicide told me about a cold case he was looking at. He opened his desk drawer and pulled out a small white envelope containing a stack of 35-millimeter photographs. He began telling me about the 1986 unsolved murder of Jennifer Bastian.

He had my full attention.

As he slowly flipped through the photos, my eyes were fixed on the horrific images. I couldn't believe what I was looking at—I was speechless. Up until this point, I had only heard about the case as a kid. Now, I was seeing what actually happened to Jennifer for the first time. Each horrifying image bombarded my imagination as I flashed back to my own childhood recollections of her murder. I thought about what this innocent little girl's last moments on earth must have been like, and it made me shudder. I wanted to cry and throw up at the same time, but of course, I didn't. That would have been considered weak, and the last thing I wanted was to have senior detectives thinking I wasn't tough enough to do the job. While these images were certainly upsetting to me, I had to keep my cool. In law enforcement, women have to work twice as hard to prove they can do the job well. There's often no room for emotion in police work, especially if you're a woman.

I learned to study murder victims, crime scenes, and photographs like Jennifer Bastian's as if they were part of a scientific experiment. This was one of the first times I remember needing to suppress my emotions so that I could do my job. I wondered how anyone could do something so violent and cruel to a child. I also knew I would never be able to forget what I had seen in those pictures.

These images, along with countless others, would consistently occupy space in my brain. I even dreamed about some of them. These images were from the worst kinds of cases imaginable—serial rapists who preyed on innocent victims, a sexual predator who broke into homes and terrorized the occupants, and children who were abducted, sexually assaulted, and murdered. As a detective, these were the cases that burrowed into my soul and changed me as a woman, a detective, a wife, and as a mother. These cases permeated the thick skin I had developed over the years, and the vivid details are now permanently intertwined with my own DNA.

CHAPTER 6

Stabbed in the Back

" *To her horror, she realized there was no interior door handle on the passenger side of the truck."*

LISA DELGADO – NOVEMBER 2, 2004

I hadn't been in sex crimes very long when I was assigned a case involving an assault on a sixteen-year-old girl named Lisa Delgado, who said she was picked up by a white male driving a small tan pickup truck three days earlier.

Lisa said she was approached by an unknown man in his truck at the Lakewood Town Center. The man offered her a ride, and she accepted. Lisa asked the man to drive her to the area of 15th and Tacoma Avenue, and he agreed. As they drove, the man asked her how old she was, and Lisa told him she was fifteen. He also asked her if she was working, and Lisa told him she didn't know what he was talking about. When they got to the area of 23rd and Tacoma Avenue on the outskirts of the Hilltop neighborhood, the man pulled out a large kitchen knife and said, "Take off your pants." Lisa didn't remove her clothing. She started crying and told the man, "I'll do what you want, just don't hurt me." The man continued to drive, and at about 25th and Tacoma Avenue, he again told her to take off her pants, and she said no. The man told her he would hurt her if she didn't do it. Lisa said the man tried to rip her pants off himself and told her, "I need to fuck some young pussy." Lisa tried to exit the vehicle, but to her horror, she realized there was no interior door handle on the passenger side of the truck. She rolled down the window and attempted to climb out, but the suspect grabbed Lisa by the leg. She was able to kick him several times, but he managed to stab Lisa in the lower back before she escaped. Lisa flagged down a passing vehicle and was taken to the hospital by the motorist.

A patrol officer took a report, but the suspect wasn't identified. Lisa's injury was fairly minor, as stab wounds go. According to the report, the suspect was a heavy-set white male in his 30s, with a round face and bulging eyes.

Aside from the high level of violence used on the victim, the missing door handle troubled me. If this report was accurate, I believed the driver of this truck probably had many more victims out there.

I discussed the case with Detective Gene Miller, who also worked sex crimes at the time. There were several similar unsolved rapes of sex workers that had occurred over the previous few years. Detective Miller told me that he'd received a call from a Pierce County Sheriff Deputy, who said he had the name of a possible suspect in my case. Pleasantly surprised, I contacted the deputy to find out what he could tell me. He said he routinely read the incident recap put out by the Law Enforcement Support Agency and learned of my case. He also said that he'd located a Field Information Report (FIR) from June 2004 involving a man named Delbert Paul Michaelson that I should look at.

I pulled up the FIR on my computer, which was dated June 22, 2004, at 1 AM. The narrative read: "Had prostitute, toy gun, 12 in butcher knife and tape in vehicle stopped by Tribal. Similar to Serial Rapist." The tribal officers also observed three-foot-long strips of masking tape adhering to the headliner of the truck. Hmmm...This guy was rolling around with a sex worker and what sounded like a rape kit in his truck—he had my full attention.

The name of the person contacted on the card was Delbert Michaelson. The truck he drove was listed as a tan 1996 Toyota pickup, and the location of the stop was a well-known hotspot for drugs and prostitution. The officer ran Michaelson for warrants and, after finding him clear, had released him. This lead sounded promising.

I ran a background check on Michaelson and found that he not only fit the description provided by Lisa Delgado, he had also been arrested in 1993 for Rape 1st Degree, and Unlawful Imprisonment. I requested a copy of the police report from archives and found that he had been arrested for an attack on a sixteen-year-old girl named Gina Smith in 1993.

GINA SMITH - SEPTEMBER 30, 1993

At 2:32 AM, Tacoma Police Officers were dispatched to the 3100 block of North 26th Street for a report of a woman screaming, possible domestic. Upon arrival, the officers located a half-naked, hysterical sixteen-year-old female in the street. Her dress was pulled down to her waist, exposing her breasts, and a black cord had been tied around her right wrist. The girl had a fresh cut on her lower lip as well. The officers also encountered a man in the street, sweating profusely, standing right behind the girl. He was later identified as Delbert Michaelson.

Both the girl and Michaelson were placed into separate patrol cars and asked to recount what happened. The girl, identified as Gina Smith, eventually told officers that she had been picked up by Michaelson in front of the Valley Motel on Puyallup Avenue.

Michaelson paid her forty dollars for sex, and she agreed to go to his apartment. When the transaction was over, Gina tried to leave, but Michaelson said he wanted more. He pulled out a small silver pistol with white grips from under his bed and pointed it at Gina's head. He tied her wrists behind her back with a cord from her dress, blindfolded her with a green tee-shirt, and forced her into the living room, where he made her perform sex acts on him.

At some point, Gina was able to push Michaelson into a glass coffee table, which shattered on impact. She ran out the front door naked. Michaelson followed and attempted to coax her back inside with an offer of returning her clothes. Gina refused and demanded that he give her back her belongings. Michaelson threw her clothing outside the apartment, where she retrieved them. The police showed up moments later after a neighbor called in the disturbance.

Michaelson's story didn't make much sense. He told the officers that he picked Gina up downtown and brought her back to his apartment, but he had no idea she wanted him to pay for sex. He said they did have sex, then she "freaked out." He told the officers that Gina wanted it rough, and while he did have a gun in the apartment, he never took it out.

Outside the apartment, the officers found a torn green tee shirt with a knot in it. Inside, they saw a shattered glass table in the living room. They also found a silver .22 caliber semi-automatic pistol with white grips lying on the bathroom sink next to Gina's earrings. In the bedroom, the officers located a condom wrapper on the floor next to the magazine for the .22 caliber pistol, which contained six rounds of ammunition.

Michaelson was arrested for Rape 1st Degree and Unlawful Imprisonment and booked into the Pierce County Jail. Gina refused medical treatment, stating she was pregnant and that she would make an appointment with her own doctor. The rape charge never stuck—and the case was eventually dismissed.

After reviewing Michaelson's 1993 arrest report and noting his vehicle description, physical description, documented association with sex workers—plus the Field Information Report document-ing the suspicious items in his truck, I believed he was a very good suspect in the assault on Lisa Delgado. But believing someone is a good suspect isn't enough. I had to work to gather additional evidence to either link Michaelson to the crime or eliminate him.

Detective Gene Miller and I met with Lisa Delgado at Remann Hall Juvenile Detention Center on November 6, 2004, and con-ducted an in-depth recorded interview with her. During the inter-view, she described the suspect as a fat white male with green eyes. She said he wore a hat, and she thought his teeth looked fake. She described his vehicle as a small gold Toyota Pickup with a bench seat and a missing interior door handle on the passenger side. She described the knife as a large kitchen knife with a black handle containing silver screws. After hearing Lisa's account of what took place, Gene told me he had been assigned a similar case a few months prior.

SADIE JONES – MAY 9, 2004

Just after 2 AM, Tacoma Police Officers responded to a report of an injury collision in the 500 block of North 5th Street. Upon arrival, the officers found thirty-nine-year-old Sadie Jones, par-tially nude, being consoled by citizens who had come to see what had happened. Sadie appeared to be in shock, and her right hand and arm were bleeding. A piece of masking tape formed into the shape of handcuffs was attached to her right wrist.

Sadie told officers that for the past week, she had been working as a sex worker. At around 2 AM, Sadie had been in the area of 11th and Tacoma Avenue when she was approached by the suspect in his gold pickup. He told her he wanted a date, and she got into his truck. As they drove away, the suspect asked, "So we're just gonna drive to my home and fuck, right?" He also asked, "We're gonna fuck for free, right?" Sadie said no. At this point, the suspect stopped the truck in a residential neighborhood and pulled a 12-inch kitchen knife from his door pocket, and held it overhead like an ice pick. He threatened to hurt her if she didn't do what he said, stating, "If you don't do everything I tell you to do, you'll get hurt."

Sadie reached for the passenger door handle to escape but found that the entire door panel was gone and covered with plastic and duct tape. Realizing she was trapped, Sadie told the suspect she'd do whatever he wanted. He ordered her to remove her clothes and then pulled out a roll of masking tape from the door pocket. He placed the knife on his lap as he began binding Sadie's hands behind her back.

Sadie saw that the knife was in his lap, and in a split second, she grabbed onto it. They fought over the knife, and in the process, Sadie's hand and arm were cut with the blade. The suspect dragged Sadie out the driver's door into the street. She managed to grab her purse and some of her clothing before she was tossed out of the truck. As she bent over to collect her belongings, the suspect drove his truck straight at her in an attempt to run her over. Sadie was able to jump onto the hood of the truck before bouncing off into the street.

When Detective Gene Miller was assigned this case, he attempted to locate the suspect vehicle in the vicinity of the incident and had the tape examined for latent prints. It came back negative. Due to the victim's transient lifestyle, Detective Miller was unable to locate Sadie for an in-depth interview.

After discussing the similarities between Sadie's case and my case involving sixteen-year-old Lisa Delgado, Gene and I agreed the cases were likely connected and began working them together. This was a unique experience because most of the serial rape cases that I worked in my career involved the investigation of numerous cases before a suspect emerged. In this case, we had a suspect early in the investigation but needed solid evidence to link him to the crimes.

Sadie was now living out of state, so Detective Miller contacted a detective who could show her a photo lineup and collect a DNA reference sample from her. In March of 2005, Detective Miller was notified that Sadie had picked Delbert Michaelson out of the lineup.

I figured there were probably more related cases out there, so I began searching our police database for similar crimes. I spent hours teaching myself how to query different keywords that I thought might yield a lead. I searched for reports involving a brown, tan, or gold pickup, reports where a knife was used in an assault, rape, or kidnapping, and I reviewed dozens of rape and kidnapping reports. This skill would come in handy during future investigations.

As a result of my queries, I found a case from 2002 in the neighboring jurisdiction of Lakewood that was similar to Sadie and Lisa's.

On December 16, 2004, Detective Gene Miller met with Lisa Delgado at Remann Hall and showed her a photo lineup containing a picture of Delbert Michaelson. She identified Michaelson as the man who had stabbed her in the back.

That same day, I contacted Detective Mike Zaro to discuss the Lakewood case from two years earlier. I explained that I had Probable Cause to arrest Delbert Michaelson for Assault First Degree for the attack on Lisa. I explained that Michaelson had been stopped by Puyallup Tribal Police in May 2004 with a sex worker in his Toyota truck. During a search of his vehicle, a large kitchen knife, along with a BB gun pistol, were found. The vehicle and suspect descriptions matched those provided by the victim from the Lakewood case, and Michaelson's middle name was Paul, the same name the suspect referred to himself during the Lakewood assault. Detective Zaro compared a booking photo of Michaelson with the composite sketch of the suspect in his 2002 case and found them to be similar.

THE ARREST

Shortly after 11 PM the evening of December 16, 2004, Delbert Michaelson was arrested by Tacoma Police Officers based on the Probable Cause to Arrest bulletin I'd issued. Michaelson, clad in his skivvies, had been plucked from his trailer in Lakewood and transported to the Criminal Investigations Division office in the County-City Building for an interview, and his truck was impounded. Once they got to the station, an officer fetched a pair of jail pants for Michaelson to wear. I contacted Detective Zaro and asked if he wanted to interview Michaelson at TPD with Detective Brad Graham and myself.

When Detective Zaro arrived, Brad and I had already begun our interview with Michaelson. Michaelson admitted to picking up sex workers in Tacoma and said he preferred white females since he'd had a bad experience with a black sex worker in the early 1990s. Michaelson said he began picking up sex workers in the early 1990s. He said he usually picked them up near the Tacoma Dome or the train station. He said he didn't have much luck on Tacoma Avenue because the girls there were "scary" and tended to be drug-addicted. He admitted he goes by his middle name, Paul, and said he'd owned his Toyota pickup for the past five years. He claimed to suffer from blackouts due to his drinking and mental health disorder. He denied ever pulling a knife on a girl or using tape on any of the females he picked up in his truck. Michaelson said the butcher knife found in his truck by Puyallup Tribal Police was for camping and the BB gun was a Halloween prop. He began to sweat profusely when questioned about the knife.

Michaelson was asked if he ever got into physical altercations with girls in his truck. He said there was an incident around October when he picked up a girl near the library on Tacoma Avenue. He said she freaked out when she saw the broken door handle, so he rolled down the window and opened the door, and let her out.

We told Michaelson that the victim in our case reported that he cut her with a knife on her back. He was quiet for a moment, then said, "No, it didn't happen." We then asked if it was possible that it did happen when he was drunk. He said, "I don't remember any incidents that gone that far." We told him we'd have to go with the victim's version of events if he couldn't remember what happened. Michaelson began to sweat again and said, "If this is the gal I'm thinking of, she pulled a penknife and stabbed me, and I grabbed the knife from under my seat. I may have hit her as she left."

When asked why the girl pulled a penknife on him, Michaelson explained that she freaked out over the missing door handle (I can't understand why), so he wanted her out of his truck. He claimed she got angry because he didn't want to date her—at which time, she stabbed him with a penknife in the chest area. When we asked how many times he stabbed the girl, Michaelson said, "I didn't know I got her, honestly."

It turned out that Michaelson was a manager at a local restaurant, and he was living in a trailer in Lakewood. After the interview, we booked Michaelson into the Pierce County jail for Assault First Degree, Kidnapping First Degree, and Attempted Rape First Degree stemming from the encounter with Lisa Delgado.

The following day, I obtained a search warrant for Michaelson's trailer and truck. During the search of the vehicle, we found six rolls of various kinds of tape, thin white rope, and a black-handled butcher knife under the driver seat. I would describe these items as a rape kit. I also observed that the interior passenger side door handle was missing. We later removed the whole passenger door from Michaelson's truck and placed it into Evidence. The butcher knife and a portion of the bench seat cover were later sent to the crime lab for DNA testing with negative results.

During the search of Michaelson's trailer, we found the place littered with trash and debris. The living room and kitchen areas were piled high with garbage, moldy food containers, and liquor bottles. One of the detectives came up with an ingenious search technique that decreased the likelihood of contamination from whatever was lurking within the confines of the nightmarish trailer. It involved the use of the coffee table as a platform, and a golf club turned search probe which was used to move and sort items from a safe distance. The most interesting things we found were in the bedroom, which looked like something you'd see on an episode of Criminal Minds. There was a length of rope on the floor with loops at both ends, and there were dirty-looking ropes attached to three of the four corners of the bed. Also, inside the trailer, we located a men's jacket with a small hole in the chest area.

After some additional digging in the computer, I found another unsolved case from May 2000 that fit Michaelson's MO.

KAREN BROWER – MAY 26, 2000

Thirty-year-old Karen Brower reported that she had been at a bar and was walking home around 11:30 PM when she was offered a ride by an unknown white male in a small silver-blue pickup in the area of 34th and Portland Avenue. After getting into the truck, the suspect drove to a convenience store and went inside briefly. While she waited in the truck, Karen happened to look up and saw three strips of duct tape, about three feet long, stuck to the roof liner of the truck.

Once they were back on the road, Karen noticed he wasn't heading toward her house and asked him where he was going. The suspect said he was turning around, but instead, he pulled down a secluded road. He drove her to a spot and then pulled a nine to ten-inch wooden-handled knife from under the seat. The suspect told her to do what he said and that if she tried anything, she'd be dead. He duct-taped her forearms with a strip of tape from the roof liner, then pushed her onto the floorboard.

The suspect proceeded to drive to another location on the bank of the Puyallup River, where he cut off the tape and forced Karen to remove her clothing. After she did this, the suspect taped her arms behind her back and then ordered her out of the truck. He then raped her repeatedly outside. During the sexual assault, he called her a "fucking cunt and whore". Afterward, he threw her clothes out of the truck and placed a piece of duct tape over her eyes before he drove away, telling her it was his final precaution. She did not immediately report the rape, but later she saw a news story about a similar attack and decided to file a police report. Karen did not go to the hospital for a sexual assault exam, but she did lead detectives to the spot where she was raped. Karen pointed out several strips of duct tape on the ground and said she had removed them after the rape. Karen was shown a photo montage containing a possible suspect but did not pick anyone in the photos. The detective assigned to the case was unable to identify a suspect in 2000.

On December 19, 2004, I spoke to the original detective assigned to the Karen Brower case and shared the similarities between her incident and the case I was investigating involving Delbert Michaelson. The detective agreed the suspect's description and MO sounded very similar. He located Karen Brower in the Pierce County

Jail, and we paid her a visit the same day. Karen was shown a photo lineup containing a picture of Delbert Michaelson. She immediately pointed to Michaelson's photo and said, "That's him." Karen admitted that she had been engaged as a sex worker the night of the assault and that the suspect was her first customer of the night. This was the reason she didn't report the rape right away.

On December 20, 2004, Detective Zaro collected the knife and BB gun taken from Michaelson's truck by Tribal Police. Reddish smearing was observed on the blade. A presumptive test was conducted, and the blade reacted positive for the presence of blood. The crime lab identified Sadie Jones's DNA on the knife. Sadie was the woman who reported being cut by the suspect's knife during a struggle inside his truck in May 2004 in Tacoma.

After Delbert Michaelson was arrested for the assault on Lisa Delgado, Lakewood Detective Mike Zaro dug into his files and found a case from the previous month in the City of Lakewood with several similarities.

TAMARA HILLYARD – NOVEMBER 13, 2004

Lakewood Police Officers were dispatched to a possible abduction that had just occurred. Two witnesses reported seeing a yellow pickup in a ditch along the side of the road. They saw a hysterical female run in front of the truck, and she flagged down the witnesses as they were passing in their car. They picked up the woman, later identified as thirty-three-year-old Tamara Hillyard. Tamara told the witnesses that a man was trying to kill her, and they called 911. One of the witnesses said Tamara was so frightened she urinated in her pants.

Tamara told officers that she was walking to a bus stop when she was approached by a white male driving a late 80's-early 90s yellowish-brown pickup. The driver said "hi" and then exited the truck. The man approached Tamara and grabbed her by the hair, and pulled her into the passenger side of the truck.

Once they were both inside the truck, the driver pulled a knife on Tamara and said, "Don't you move bitch." The suspect drove to the 9200 block of Front Street and told Tamara it was her time to die. The driver rolled down the passenger side window and pushed Tamara out. Tamara got up and started to run, but the suspect intentionally struck her with his truck, causing her to land in a ditch beside the road.

When Tamara got up, the suspect approached on foot and struck her with a small baseball bat. Tamara said she played dead, and the suspect went back to his truck, where she heard him rifling through the contents of his vehicle. She took that opportunity to try and run away, but the suspect got back inside his truck and tried to chase her down again. This time his truck got stuck in the ditch, and Tamara was able to run into the street and flag down a passing motorist. The suspect was gone by the time police arrived.

Detective Zaro set out to find Tamara Hillyard and eventually located her in a correctional facility out of state. On January 20, 2005, he met with Tamara in the prison and showed her a photo lineup containing a picture of Delbert Michaelson. Tamara positively identified Michaelson as the man who'd attacked her in November 2004. During the interview, Tamara was asked about the suspect's vehicle. She recalled that the interior passenger door handle didn't work. She also recalled the suspect telling her, "It's your day to die, bitch."

While Delbert Michaelson sat in jail, I continued to search for more cases that could be linked to him. I found two more cases from 2001 that sounded very similar to Michaelson's MO.

Unfortunately, the victims never went to the hospital for a sexual assault exam, so there was no physical evidence, and neither of the victims was able to pick Michaelson out of a photo lineup.

Delbert Michaelson was ultimately charged with fourteen felony crimes stemming from the attacks on Lisa Delgado, Sadie Jones, Karen Brower, and Tamara Hillyard. The charges included Rape, Kidnapping, Robbery, and Assault.

Delbert Michaelson pled guilty to one count of Rape Second Degree, one count of Attempted Rape First Degree and two counts of Attempted Rape Second Degree. He was sentenced to twenty years to life in prison for his crimes. Three years after he was sent to prison, the crime lab identified Michaelson's DNA on duct tape removed from the victim's eyes in an unsolved 2002 Lakewood rape case thanks to advances in DNA testing. Although Michaelson was not charged with that case, this information could be used by the Department of Corrections end of sentence review board if Michaelson ever comes up for parole.

This investigation was extremely challenging for a number of reasons. Unlike most episodes of CSI, there was limited forensic evidence, and DNA only linked Michaelson to one of the crimes he was charged with. There was no video surveillance, fingerprints, or cell phone data. The cases were identified and linked primarily by MO, suspect description, and vehicle description. Several of the victims were able to positively identify Michaelson from photo lineups, and the suspect admitted to stabbing one of the victims at the time of his arrest.

Michaelson also preyed on the most vulnerable women in our society. Like many other serial offenders, he sought out marginalized women, many of whom struggled with drug and alcohol addiction. He chose victims who would be unlikely to report victimization to police for fear of not being believed or being arrested based on their profession. The victims were mostly living transient lifestyles with no fixed address or stable means of communication. These victims didn't have reliable transportation and didn't show up for scheduled appointments. In order to successfully prosecute these cases, we had to pound the pavement and track down our victims. We also had to convey to them that we believed them—despite their circumstances in life or what they had to do to earn a living.

Let's face it—I could have investigated the one case in this series that I was assigned and called it good. No one asked me to search out other victims, but I wanted to because I knew there were more and because I believed Delbert Michaelson was a dangerous predator who needed to go to prison for as long as possible so that he couldn't hurt anyone else. Not all detectives are willing to work so hard to solve these kinds of cases, and I believe many serial offenders count on that.

CHAPTER 7

Your Worst Nightmare

I'm tense as we make our way through the yard at the penitentiary in Walla Walla. Eyes burrow into me from every direction—restless inmates watch as Brad, and I follow the concrete path from one dismal building to the next. I'm exposed, like a piece of raw meat being dangled inside the lion enclosure at the zoo...

The first time I heard the name Donald Schneider was in February 2005. I'd been in sex crimes for close to a year at that point. Detective Gene Miller and I were given an unsavory assignment—reinvestigate several sexual assault cases previously assigned to another detective who was no longer in the unit. One of those cases turned out to be the kidnapping and rape of a fifty-three-year-old woman that occurred in McKinley Park on the east side of Tacoma the previous April.

Tacoma Police Officer Gwen Beverly was dispatched to the Puyallup Tribal Police Station, where she encountered the victim, Mary Smith. Mary was disheveled and dirty, with sticks and leaves tangled throughout her matted hair. Thick sticky lines ran across her face and wrists, indicating she'd been bound with duct tape.

Mary told the officer that she'd encountered the suspect in the area of East 28th and L, and he offered her a ride. This area was a hotbed for drug and prostitution activity at the time. Mary said she sometimes engaged as a sex worker but wasn't working that night. She said the suspect picked her up in a small white sedan, and they drove to nearby McKinley Park. They walked down a trail to a spot he chose. He laid a piece of cloth down on the ground and suddenly pulled out a knife. He told Mary to do exactly what he told her, or he would stab her in the heart and bury her right there. Mary said his voice and demeanor changed rapidly from just a few seconds before.

The suspect brutally sexually assaulted Mary, then pulled a roll of duct tape from his backpack and wrapped pieces of it around her mouth and head. He also bound her wrists behind her back with the tape. At this point, she was lying face down on the ground and could hear him rummaging around in his backpack. He said he had a toy he wanted to use on her. She never saw what it was but said it was extremely painful. When she struggled, he threatened to use a tree branch on her if she didn't cooperate.

Mary said the vicious attack went on for several hours. During that time, she was repeatedly raped. After each rape, he squirted some kind of liquid into her, saying it was cleansing gel. The suspect mumbled incoherently and scattered the contents of his backpack around the area as he dug through it. He also tore up groundcover and shrubs that he fashioned into a makeshift bed. He gave Mary a handful of pills and told her to chew them up; then, he pulled out a small bottle of Scope mouthwash from his backpack for her to drink in order to wash the pills down. When he wasn't looking, she spit them out and rolled on top of them in an attempt to conceal what she'd done. The man told Mary that he was recently released from prison and that he was getting treatment at a nearby mental health facility. He also told her he was driving his mother's car.

The suspect used his knife to cut the duct tape off Mary. He tied a shoelace to her wrist and his and then laid down on the pile of vegetation to rest. Apparently, kidnapping, binding, and raping someone is tiring work. Eventually, he decided they should leave.

"I am a sick bastard," he said.

He told her he wasn't going to kill her and that she was lucky he wasn't Bundy. He warned Mary not to work as a prostitute anymore. Then the suspect drove Mary to the corner of 34th and Portland Ave, where she got out and walked home.

Mary didn't plan to seek medical attention or call the police because she thought she'd be in trouble since she sometimes engaged in sex work. After taking one look at her, Mary's roommate convinced her to go to the police.

Mary was able to lead officers to McKinley Park, and she described the steep trail leading to the crime scene. Officers located the scene and found Mary's shorts and bra, which appeared to have been cut or torn up. They found the cloth the suspect made Mary lie down on, along with several pieces of cut duct tape, a roll of duct tape, a shoestring, an empty Vaseline container, an empty bottle of Scope mouthwash, and an empty bottle of OxyClean.

Mary was taken to Tacoma General Hospital, where a Sexual Assault Nurse Examiner (SANE) completed a rape kit. While Mary was being tended to, Officer Beverly made inquiries with local medical facilities about the pills given to Mary by the suspect. She was able to identify the medication based on the description provided by Mary.

Officer Beverly came up with the name Donald Schneider after conducting a search for registered sex offenders in the area. She checked with the Department of Corrections and learned he was a level 3 violent registered sex offender and that his mother lived on East Wright Street, which was less than a half-mile from Mckinley Park. He was recently in jail for a probation violation, was receiving mental health treatment at the same facility named by the suspect, and was prescribed the drug described by Mary. Schneider's mother owned a small white sedan similar to the vehicle described by Mary, as well.

The original detective assigned to the case showed Mary a photo lineup containing a picture of Donald Schneider, but she wasn't able to identify him. During Mary's interview with the detective, she told him the suspect wore gold wire-framed glasses. Her rape kit was sent to the Washington State Patrol Crime Lab for DNA testing, and a request for latent print examination was made for some of the items collected from the crime scene. No prints were located.

Mary's case was reassigned to me in February 2005. After reading the reports associated with the horrifying case, I did a background check on Donald Schneider and found a lengthy criminal history. He was listed as a forty-five-year-old white male, 6'2, 240 pounds, with short blondish brown hair and blue eyes.

Donald Schneider's first documented sex offense was on March 23, 1982, in Tacoma. He was twenty-four at the time. The victim was a fourteen-year-old white female named Jessica Frame. Jessica reported that she was walking alone in the area of East 38th and McKinley Avenue when she noticed an unknown man—later identified as Donald Schneider—slow down and stare at her, then drive past.

Schneider pulled around the block and parked his car before approaching the girl on foot. When she noticed him exit his vehicle, Jessica pulled out a pocket knife to protect herself. She began walking quickly, and when she turned around to see where he was, she saw that Schneider was running towards her. At this point, Schneider charged at her and knocked her to the ground, taking the knife from her. He punched Jessica repeatedly and slammed her head into the pavement. When she tried to yell for help, Schneider held the knife to her and said, "If you do not stop fighting, I'll kill you." Then he dragged her up a nearby incline to a grassy area where he raped her.

During the assault, Jessica's screams were heard by nearby residents who called police. Officers responded to the area and began to investigate. As they searched the area for the source of the disturbance, they came upon Schneider in the act of raping the girl. The officers ordered Schneider to freeze, but instead, he jumped up and tried to make a run for it. He didn't get far before he tripped over his pants, which had been around his ankles.

After he was taken into custody, one of the officers told Schneider he came close to being shot. Schneider replied, "You should have."

After her terrifying ordeal, Jessica Frame was treated at the hospital for her injuries and later released. Donald Schneider was booked into the Pierce County Jail for Rape First Degree. He eventually pled guilty to Rape Second Degree and was sentenced to ten years in prison.

In January 1998, Schneider was arrested for attempting to steal a car at knifepoint in a convenience store parking lot. Upon his arrest, the police found several pornographic magazines and a bottle of lotion in his possession. The explanation provided by Schneider was that he was single, and it was better than hurting someone. There were no other documented sex crimes for Schneider between the 1982 rape and the 2004 rape.

As I continued my investigation into the 2004 rape of Mary Smith, I found a 2003 booking photo of Donald Schneider wearing gold wire-framed eyeglasses. Schneider had been booked into jail dozens of times, and in each photo, he looked completely different. He was a true chameleon.

I wanted to find out if the rape kit had been tested, so I contacted the DNA Supervisor at the Washington State Patrol Crime Lab and discussed the case with him. He advised that the rape kit had been submitted but not yet tested. He requested that I also submit the cloth that Mary had been sitting on at the scene.

In April 2005, I received notification from the crime lab that there was a match to semen in the rape kit and the cloth to Donald Schneider. Four days later, I obtained a search warrant for Schneider's apartment and his mother's car. We asked the Pierce County Sheriff's Department Sex Offender Registration Unit to call Schneider into the County-City Building for a meeting. When he arrived (with his mom), Detective Gene Miller and I arrested him. We took him to an interview room in the Criminal Investigations Division.

During the interview, I studied Schneider closely. I'd arrested many men over the years and rarely felt intimidated by them, but there was something about this man that made the hair on the back of my neck stand up. The same kind of feeling Gavin de Becker described in his book *The Gift of Fear*, where he discussed survival signals or instincts that humans often ignore.

We questioned Schneider about the rape and kidnapping of Mary Smith. Schneider denied raping anyone but admitted to meeting a "hooker" at the AM/PM on Puyallup Avenue and taking her to McKinley Park, where they did "pretty much everything." He said it was a consensual deal for $30 and that "She acted like she wanted to get rough." He claimed she wanted him to pull her hair and choke her—but he didn't. He also said he hadn't been violent with anyone for a long time. Schneider denied using duct tape and said if it was involved, then she would have brought it. When we asked if the woman had any injuries, he said, "I didn't see them if she did."

After the interview, we booked Schneider into the Pierce County Jail for Rape First Degree and Kidnapping First Degree. After the case was charged, I spent a lot of time trying to keep track of Mary Smith. She was living a transient lifestyle, so getting in touch with her was difficult.

In January 2007, Schneider was found guilty at trial of Rape

First Degree and Unlawful Imprisonment and sentenced to life without the possibility of parole, thanks to Washington's two strikes law for sex offenses. Many states, including Washington, have a three-strikes law for violent felony convictions, but offenders in Washington convicted of certain sex crimes receive a mandatory life sentence without the possibility of parole upon a second conviction.

During the follow-up investigation into Schneider's past, I learned of a troubling incident that reportedly occurred around 1993. According to Schneider's ex-wife, Linda, she and a red-headed schoolmate we'll call "Jane" went to a motel with Schneider and another man to party. The two girls were about thirteen at the time, and both men were adults. At some point during the evening, Jane said she wanted to go home. Schneider told Linda that he had taken Jane home. Linda said that Jane's mother called a couple of days later asking if she'd seen her daughter. Linda said Schneider told her that he had dropped Jane off at home. Linda never saw Jane again.

Linda couldn't recall the name of the girl and thought she was new to her school that year. I spent months attempting to identify Jane. I had Linda look through yearbooks with no success. I searched missing persons and runaway records and asked for help from the National Center for Missing and Exploited Children. Unfortunately, juveniles who were reported missing or runaway in the '70s and '80s were considered emancipated when they turned eighteen and were usually purged from the National Crime Information Center (NCIC). I still have no idea if the mystery redhead was another one of Schneider's victims.

I figured that was the end of the Donald Schneider's story, but it wasn't.

In July 2011, I was researching sex crimes and kidnapping reports in our old report indexing system called CLEAR, looking for any cases that might be linked to the 1986 unsolved murder of Jennifer Bastian or a 1999 child abduction case I was working. My former partner, Detective Gene Miller, was the cold case detective at that time, and although I wasn't assigned to the cold case unit then, I did work on a few cold cases as time allowed. This wasn't mandatory, but I had always been interested in cold cases and wanted to work on a couple in the hopes that I might find the answers. Typically, I would start by reading through the case from start to finish, usually more than once. I would make notes on a legal pad and attach yellow post-it notes to significant pages. I would examine the crime scene and autopsy photos in an attempt to understand how the crime was committed, and I would go to the crime scene to get a feel for the area since I didn't have the advantage of being there when the crime occurred. My review of items collected as evidence was critical. I would check to see what, if anything, had been tested at the crime lab and then make a to-do list which often included locating witnesses and suspects (if they were still alive) and determining what if anything warranted fingerprint examinations or DNA, firearms, or trace analysis at the crime lab. Old VHS tapes and audio tapes had to be converted into digital format, and so did the crime scene photos, which were usually 35mm.

At that time, my old partner and I had an understanding that I would do whatever I could to assist on the Jennifer Bastian case. One of the cases I found during my search of the CLEAR database was the 1995 kidnapping and rape of a nine-year-old girl in Buckley, WA. Buckley is a small rural town in unincorporated Pierce County, about twenty miles east of Tacoma.

I read through all of the reports associated with the investigation and learned that on the morning of September 20, 1995, nine-year-old Emily Pierce was walking to her school bus stop. She was approached by an unknown man in a small yellow car who asked her for the time. As Emily got closer to the car, the man grabbed her and forced her inside. The man told Emily he had a knife and threatened to kill her if she wasn't quiet. He pushed her down on the passenger floorboard and covered her with a jacket. After driving a short distance, the man pulled over and used duct tape to bind Emily's hands behind her back; he stuffed a rag into her mouth and then duct-taped her mouth shut.

The man drove to a wooded area near the town of Eatonville. The man led Emily into the woods, where he brutally sexually assaulted her. After the assault, he told Emily, "I'm a drunk old man, and my brain needs help." He warned her by saying, "Don't tell, or I'll come back 'cause I know where you live, and I'll kill your family and even you." Before he left, the man told Emily to count to 100, and then she could get dressed and leave.

Emily was able to find her way to the highway and was picked up by a passing motorist. She was taken to Mary Bridge Children's Hospital in Tacoma, where she was treated for her injuries which required surgical repair. Pierce County Sheriff's Deputies located the crime scene, and Emily was able to help create a composite sketch of the suspect.

The Sheriff's Department devoted considerable resources to the investigation, and they received tips on more than thirty possible suspects, including a man who'd been shot by a farmer in the rural town of Enumclaw after he was caught having sex with a goat. Despite the investigative efforts at the time, the suspect was never apprehended.

As I read through the case, I was shocked by the brutality of the crime. I had a sick feeling in my gut, thinking about what little Emily had to endure. My own nine-year-old daughter was sitting across from me, stringing together beaded friendship bracelets as I wrote this—I can't even begin to imagine something so horrifying happening to her.

I read through the property reports and saw that a rape kit was collected at the hospital in 1995. I didn't find any corresponding lab reports indicating there had been DNA testing done during the investigation. I called the Pierce County Property Room and asked if the rape kit had ever been sent to the crime lab. No. My next step was to find out if the rape kit was still in evidence or if it had been destroyed. I was in luck. The kit had been maintained.

I reached out to Pierce County Sheriff Cold Case Detective Tim Kobel and told him about Emily's case and her untested rape kit. I asked if he would submit it to the Crime Lab for DNA testing. The reason for this was two-fold: I thought there was the possibility that the DNA from Emily's rape kit might match the DNA from the Michella Welch case. And even if it didn't, whoever kidnapped and raped Emily was a dangerous sexual predator who needed to be identified and locked up.

And so, the waiting began. Something you get used to working cold cases. The normal turnaround time for DNA testing at the Crime Lab was six months to a year, depending on the priority level of your submission.

Finally, in February 2012, I got a call from Detective Kobel—there was a CODIS hit in Emily's case. The unknown male DNA from her underwear matched a previously convicted felon in the database. Donald Victor Schneider.

Holy shit.

Detective Kobel told me the crime lab also notified him of a match between the offender DNA profile from the 2004 Mary Smith case and the evidence in Emily's case. This is called a case-to-case match in CODIS. Law enforcement agencies around the country are notified if the DNA profile from their case matches a DNA profile from another case, even if the identity of the offender is unknown.

I was stunned when I found out Schneider was responsible for

Emily's abduction and rape. I guess it explained the gap between 1982 and 2004 in his criminal history. With most sexual predators, we typically only find out about a small percentage of the crimes the offender actually committed throughout his life.

When I burst into Gene Miller's office and told him the news, he couldn't believe it either. Gene and Detective Kobel traveled to the Washington State Penitentiary in Walla Walla to interview Schneider. I was recovering from rotator cuff surgery at the time, so I couldn't go. Schneider didn't talk, but a fresh sample of his DNA was collected to confirm the CODIS hit.

Schneider was charged with Rape First Degree and Rape of a Child First Degree and was brought back to Pierce County to await his trial. In 2013, he pled guilty to Rape of a Child First Degree and was sentenced to life in prison without parole for the second time.

After he was charged with Emily's case, I reached out to the National Center for Missing and Exploited Children (NCMEC) and asked them to dig up anything they could find on Schneider. I wanted to find out if he could be linked to any other cold cases. While his previous crimes certainly made me consider him for Jennifer Bastian's case, I knew he wasn't responsible for her murder because he was in prison when the crime occurred, and his DNA is in CODIS. I asked NCMEC to create a timeline that would incorporate any documented contacts with law enforcement, Department of Corrections, employment history, vehicle registration history, and address history. Any time his name was queried by law enforcement for a warrant check from 1990 to present, anywhere in the US was included as well. Also included were cases in the NCMEC database that matched Schneider's MO. I also searched the FBI's Violent Criminal Apprehension Program (ViCAP) database and our state Homicide Investigation Tracking System (HITS) database looking for associated cases. Once the timeline was completed, I shared it with other cold case detectives in Washington.

There are two other cases I found that sound strikingly similar to Schneider's MO, but neither of the cases will ever be prosecuted. The first occurred on July 30, 2004, just three months after the rape of Mary Smith in McKinley Park. It was 8 PM on a warm summer night when eleven-year-old Holly Chambers and her mother Michelle were out walking in the area of 67th and A street in Tacoma. Suddenly, a man jumped out from behind a hedge and said, "Hello, ladies."

The man grabbed Holly and pushed her mother out of the way as he pulled a butcher knife from behind his back. Michelle and Holly fought with the knife-wielding man, and Holly was able to break free from his grasp. The man ran to a blue 1980's Datsun pickup with a wooden box in the bed parked nearby and sped out of the area.

Holly and Michelle were able to help create a composite sketch of the suspect. When the sketch was broadcast on the local news, a detective with the Snohomish County Sheriff's Office, about seventy miles north of Tacoma, believed he recognized the sketch as a recently released sex offender who lived in Snohomish County. This man was eventually arrested and charged for the attempted abduction of Holly Chambers, but the trial resulted in a hung jury.

While the prosecution was gearing up for a retrial, I was assigned the Mary Smith rape case from McKinley Park. When I pulled up Donald Schneider's booking photo for the first time, I was shocked at the striking similarity between his photo and the composite sketch from the Holly Chambers case. One of his 2005 booking photos even showed him wearing rectangular lens eyeglasses, just like the ones in the composite sketch.

I showed the photo to the detective working the Holly Chambers case, and he was stunned. After a little more digging, we found that Schneider owned a truck similar to the one described by Holly and Michelle, but he reported it stolen after the attack. According to Schneider, he collected wooden pallets for money and hauled them in the bed of his truck. He bore a striking resemblance to the sketch, and he didn't live far from the site of the attempted abduction. The blitz attack was very similar to the abduction and rape of Jessica Frame in 1982.

The similarities between Schneider and the suspect from the Holly Chambers case were discussed with the prosecutor. Eventually, the circumstantial case against the Snohomish County sex offender was dismissed, but there wasn't enough evidence to charge Schneider with the crime either.

The other case that I found happened on November 25, 1988. Once again, I'd been digging out old cases from the archives, looking for any similarities to the unsolved 1986 murder of Jennifer Bastian, when I came across a very disturbing report.

Two fourteen-year-old girls, Amanda Lacey and Roberta Flynn had just gotten off of a bus on 288th near Pacific Highway in Federal Way, just north of Tacoma. They noticed an unknown male in a dark blue Chevy Nova honk his horn and then pass by them. As the girls approached a brushy area, the driver of the Nova jumped out from behind the bushes and grabbed one of the girls by the throat. He was armed with a knife and forced both girls into the Nova. He drove the frightened teens more than eighteen miles through the Tacoma tide flats to McKinley Park on the Eastside of Tacoma (this is the same park where Schneider took Mary Smith in 2004).

The girls recalled that the man told them he wasn't a child molester as he drove them to the park. They noticed the passenger side door handle had been removed, so they couldn't get out of the car. [Side note: Is there some kind of serial rapist playbook these guys study? The missing door handle routine was one of the tactics used by serial rapist Delbert Michaelson to trap his victims in his truck.] Once they arrived at the park, the man pulled out a roll of duct tape from his backpack and taped their hands behind their backs and taped their mouths shut. He led the girls into the wooded park and sexually assaulted both of them. Afterward, he told the girls that drugs made him do it. He told Amanda and Roberta to lie on the ground for twenty minutes, then go to the Tacoma Dome where someone would help them.

The girls eventually made their way to a nearby residence, and Tacoma Police were called. Both girls were taken to the hospital, and a composite sketch was created of the suspect. No arrests were ever made in the case.

While reading the report, I recognized many similarities to Schneider's MO. I obtained the crime scene photos and pictures taken of Amanda and Roberta at the hospital, showing their injuries. I checked with the Pierce County Property Room to see if any evidence from the 1988 rapes remained, but it had all been destroyed.

DNA testing was in its infancy in 1988, and a primitive form of DNA testing called Restriction Fragment Length Polymorphism (RFLP) was not a service offered at the Washington State Patrol Crime Lab until 1989. While a DNA profile could be obtained using this method, there was no DNA database to compare evidence samples to offenders until 2000 in Washington State. Unless you had a suspect's DNA to compare to your evidence, a DNA profile was basically useless.

Even though there was no physical evidence, I felt it was important to reach out to the victims. I had concerns about reopening old wounds twenty-five years after the fact, especially since I didn't have good news to share. I never interviewed Roberta, but I located a phone number for Amanda and reached out to her by phone. When I introduced myself and explained the reason for my call, there was silence. Then I could hear Amanda crying.

I immediately regretted the call and felt terrible for bringing that horrible experience back up to the surface again for her. I apologized for calling out of the blue, but before I could finish, Amanda surprised me. She composed herself and told me she was crying because she was happy. Happy that someone cared about what happened to her and that she hadn't been forgotten.

Wow. That was powerful. Even while writing this so many years later, I felt my throat tightening, and my eyes began to water as I recalled that conversation. It was one of those moments when I knew that what I did for a living really mattered. The times I was able to provide a grieving parent with hope or demonstrate to a victim that they weren't forgotten were the most rewarding times of my career.

Detective Brad Graham and I met with Amanda at her home. We showed her a series of photos, including one of Donald Schneider, but she wasn't able to recognize anyone. I wasn't optimistic—it had been twenty-five years since the abduction and rape. Still, it was worth it to talk to Amanda and express our desire to follow up on the case, even if we couldn't arrest anyone.

Several years later, in October 2015, Brad and I sat down with Schneider at the Washington State Penitentiary in Walla Walla. We were there to interview two other inmates after their DNA linked them to two previously untested rape kits, so we decided to stop in and say hi to him.

As a female, walking through the yard at Walla Walla is an experience. All eyes are on you. I didn't want to know what the gawking inmates were thinking, but I suspect they weren't pleasant thoughts.

When we met with Schneider, I hoped he would be willing to discuss the 1988 abduction and rape of Amanda Lacey and Roberta Flynn. I also hoped to discuss the attempted abduction of Holly Chambers in 2004.

To my surprise, Schneider was fairly pleasant to talk to once we assured him we weren't there to slap new charges on him. I asked if he remembered me from 2005. It took him a few seconds before a slight look of recognition appeared on his face. Then he said, "Oh yeah...you changed your hair."

He told us that he had done a lot of bad things in his life, and he deserved to be in prison. When we asked about the two cases, he said he didn't recall either one. He said his memory was terrible due to his prolonged Methamphetamine use. I asked if he would be willing to talk again in the future about his methods, victim selection, etc. He seemed agreeable but indicated it would have to be after his mother passed away—he didn't want her seeing him on the news again.

I hope I get a chance to talk with Schneider again. His nightmarish crimes were brutal and terrifying, but I believe there is much more to learn from this man. He was the real-life boogeyman.

CHAPTER 8

True Evil

*I*t's 2005, and the public is terrified. There's a dangerous sexual predator on the loose, and no one can predict when or where he'll strike next.

I'm consumed with the case, and my anxiety seems to ratchet up as the days go on. I'm having trouble sleeping and consider stashing a gun under my pillow. This guy is so brazen that it seems no one is immune.

In reality, I live in the middle of nowhere, and in the words of Mr. T—I pity the fool who makes the mistake of breaking into my house. Nevertheless, my husband Ed is heading off to Eastern Washington for a hunting trip, so I tell him to go to Home Depot and get wooden dowels for all the windows and doors before he leaves because clearly, the gated community and alarm system aren't good enough.

Now that the house is up to Fort Knox standards, I only feel the need to sleep with my gun on my nightstand instead of under my pillow.

Shortly after I transferred to the Special Assault Unit (SAU) in 2004, I began working closely with Detectives Gene Miller and Brad Graham. There were only six of us working sex crimes and child abuse cases back then. For the first few months, I was in the unit; Brad was in Polygraph school down in California. There was no real training for new detectives; they handed me a detective badge and started assigning me cases. The standard marching orders were, "If you have questions, ask." I took advantage of all the free training I could find, and I applied for and got approved to attend several great training classes out of state.

At that time, the Criminal Investigations Division was on the 4th floor of the County City Building in downtown Tacoma. The building housed both Tacoma Municipal and Pierce County Superior Courts, along with the Pierce County Prosecutor's Office and both the Tacoma Police Department and the Pierce County Sheriff's Department. The county jail was attached to the building. On a fairly regular basis, I would make my way up to Mary Robnett's office on the 10th floor and park myself in the chair next to her desk. Mary was a tough deputy prosecutor in charge of the Special Assault Unit at that time, and even though she was busy, she was always willing to go through my cases with me and give me her opinion. She was a great mentor and role model to me.

I was fortunate to have Brad and Gene to work with. They were both older and had many more years of experience than I did but never treated me like a rookie. They answered all my questions, and I learned a great deal from them. Gene was a taskmaster. I don't think he allowed many people to break through his tough exterior, but I was fortunate enough to be one of the few.

When it came to working cases, he was like a dog with a bone. One summer, we worked a serial rape case involving what turned out to be a disgruntled "John" who started committing violent rapes on sex workers after getting his ass kicked and robbed by a lady of the night. In one of the attacks, he anally raped a woman with a screwdriver. We spent weeks on surveillance along the South Tacoma Way corridor, trying to catch the guy. The rapist was eventually identified by an astute patrol officer. You get to know a person pretty well when you spend hours on end together in a hot car. Gene could be abrasive at times, but he was driven to seek the truth and cared about the victims in his cases—regardless of their lifestyle choices.

I'll never forget one of the first child abuse cases we worked together. A woman and her boyfriend brought their baby to the hospital with bruises all over his face and head. I was furious when I saw the photos and wasted no time tracking down the mother and her partner. They had no explanation for the injuries other than, "The ghosts must have done it." Seriously? I was beginning to understand just how cruel parents and caregivers could be to the children they were entrusted to care for. As time went on, I wasn't surprised when a suspect would tell me how their baby fell off a couch or a bed and ended up with a massive skull fracture and brain damage. Highly unlikely, unless, of course, the bed was on the roof of a three-story building, and the kid landed on concrete. We came to recognize this pathetic fabrication as the *killer bed* or *killer couch* explanation.

Gene transferred to the homicide unit in 2005, but we still worked together often. At that time, we had permanent callout teams. We got called out for homicides and home invasion rapes. Sometimes we got called out if there was a life-threatening assault where it looked like the victim was going to die. We also got called for attended suicides and infant deaths. We were on the hook for all officer-involved shootings too. The callout teams consisted of three rotating teams of four detectives, two from homicide and two from Special Assaults. Our callout team consisted of Detectives Gene Miller and Dave Devault from Homicide and Detective Brad Graham and me from Special Assaults. Each team was on call for two weeks, then off for four weeks.

Brad and I just clicked, and he soon became like a brother to me. We worked so many cases together and had fun doing it—his dry sense of humor is second to none. Brad is the best interviewer I have ever worked with. The key to interviewing is being a good listener. You can let a person ramble on and pick up all kinds of tidbits that you can use to build themes later. Once, a suspect tried to convince us of his innocence by saying, "I love Shannon...I'd drink her bathwater." Um, ok. Another time, a suspect told us he couldn't have raped the victim because he'd heard she had the "cherry popping test," and it showed nothing happened to her. Not exactly a rocket scientist.

When it comes to interviewing, it pays to be yourself. Trying to be someone else never works out, and most people can tell if you're faking it. Brad was a former US Marine with quick wit, but he showed genuine compassion for victims of the crimes he investigated. After the service, he joined the Santa Ana Police Department. He spent a couple of years patrolling the streets of Southern California before moving to Washington and joining the Tacoma Police Department in 1989. I should point out that I was in the 8th grade in 1989.

As a proud Chicago native who loves The Cubs and authentic deep-dish pizza, Brad was always disgusted when I ordered pineapple on mine—according to him, fruit has no business on a pizza. One childhood memory he shared over the years included being repulsed by dead fish he saw floating in the Chicago River—he doesn't touch seafood. Another was having to hand over his lunch money to the Vice Lords on a regular basis on his way to school. One of his endearing qualities would be his propensity to swap random syllables in words and names. For example, Officer Lorberau became Officer Lowenbrau. Brad's Chicago accent has something to do with that, I'm sure.

One of the first serious child abuse cases Brad and I worked together involved a newborn who'd been shaken by his father. The baby presented at Mary Bridge Children's Hospital with a skull fracture and subdural hematoma. The infant had been treated in the emergency department previously for vomiting and diarrhea. All of this information led doctors to suspect Shaken Baby Syndrome—now referred to as Abusive Head Trauma.

Brad and I interrogated the father at the station, and he eventually confessed to shaking the baby because he wouldn't stop crying. In those days, we didn't have video recording available in our interview rooms, so we borrowed a video camera from Forensics and set it up in the doorway of the interview room. We asked the man to recreate the incident using a baby doll. He agreed and began shaking the doll during his demonstration.

I asked the man if his portrayal of the assault accurately demonstrated the force he used when he shook the infant. He replied, no, he had shaken his son much harder. At that point, he picked up the doll and shook it so hard that the head whipped back and forth violently, and the little cotton hat flew off its head. He finished by smacking the doll's head on the table to demonstrate how he slammed his son's head into a dresser.

After the interview, we told the man he was going to jail for the assault on his son. He wasn't surprised. The thing I remember most is that he asked Brad for a hug when we were done. I guess that's what you call rapport building.

We spent too many hours in the Pediatric Intensive Care Unit (PICU) at Mary Bridge Children's Hospital over the years. For some reason, people seemed to be more prone to brutalizing kids in the winter months. I'd undoubtedly be dressed in a turtleneck sweater on a day we got sent to the PICU on a case. It felt like a sauna in that unit, and I used to call that time of year "turtleneck season."

Brad and I interviewed a lot of suspects over the years, and most of them were men. Some of these guys didn't even try to hide their annoyance with being questioned by a female cop. During one interaction, the suspect referred to me as "the girl cop." It didn't faze me, but it must have stuck with Brad because, after that, he would occasionally greet me in the morning with a chipper, "Hi, girl cop." From anyone else, this would have come off as sexist and demeaning, but from Brad, I took it as a term of endearment. It was another one of the many inside jokes we shared over the years.

We also spent a lot of time at the Children's Advocacy Center (CAC), where children who disclosed physical or sexual abuse were taken for forensic interviews. This is where I met one of my closest friends, Amy Scanlon. She was a Child Protection Services social worker who was assigned to the CAC. She later married another one of my close friends, Detective Brad Graham.

October 2005 was a busy time for the Tacoma Police Department. We were in the process of moving into our new headquarters building in the 3700 block of South Pine—the old Tacoma Costco site (we called it COPCO for the first couple of years). The Patrol Division was moving from the ramshackle station located at 38th and Puget Sound while the rest of the department, including the Criminal Investigations Division, was clearing out our tired digs on the 3rd and 4th floors of the County-City Building.

October 9, 2005, was a damp and gloomy fall day in Tacoma. Early that Sunday morning, Gene Miller and I were called out to a home invasion rape that occurred overnight.

I arrived at an ordinary-looking two-story house on South Trafton Street, just off 6th Avenue. Three young roommates shared the house. The crime scene investigation was already underway. The exterior phone line to the residence had been cut, and it looked like the suspect made entry through a basement window. After a quick walk-through, Gene and I headed to the hospital and left another detective in charge of processing the crime scene.

At the hospital, I made contact with the responding officers, who provided me with an overview of what they'd learned so far.

The primary officer was skeptical of the seemingly outrageous story. Just like in the Netflix series *Unbelievable*, sometimes the most outrageous things really do happen. One of the victims, Amy Williams, called 911 from her ex-boyfriend's house to report the incident. She told the 911 dispatcher that an unknown man wearing a mask and armed with a gun had broken into their house in the middle of the night and sexually assaulted her. After several hours, the suspect left, and they fled to her ex's house.

I spoke to Amy's two roommates, Kara and Lauren, at the hospital and learned that an unknown man entered their home in the middle of the night. He demanded money and tied up two of the three women in the home. He forced them into a bedroom closet, then the bathroom, using the cords from a clothes iron and flat irons as restraints. He forced Amy to cover their heads with pillowcases. Kara and Lauren were corralled in the bathroom while their friend Amy was repeatedly raped.

I spoke to Amy briefly at the hospital. She was clearly in shock and exhibited a flat affect with no visible emotion. To the untrained observer, Amy's lack of hysteria might have been mistaken for a false claim of rape. I had already investigated dozens of rapes, including two terrifying serial rapists by that point in my career, and I knew from experience that traumatized victims aren't always visibly upset. I had no doubt that something terrible had happened to these women. I got some basic information from Amy about potential evidence that might be at her house so the crime scene could be processed immediately. She told me the suspect forced her to bathe and brush her teeth after the rapes. The green and white toothbrush she used would be in the shower. I decided not to attempt a complete interview with Amy that day based on the amount of time she would spend at the hospital and the trauma she'd endured.

Back in 2005, I hadn't been trained on the effects of trauma on the brain. This concept is particularly applicable in cases of sexual assault. When a person undergoes a traumatic event, like a sexual assault, their body goes into survival mode. Most people are familiar with the concept of FIGHT or FLIGHT, but what you may not have heard about is the third option—FREEZE.

FREEZE, also known as tonic immobility, is an involuntary response to a life or death situation. This is a defense mechanism and the brain's way of keeping you alive. With sexual assault, people often blame the victim for putting themselves in a position to be raped or blame them for not fighting off the attacker.

A common fallacy goes something like this, "If someone tried to rape me, I'd scream and fight back." We'd all like to think we would do whatever it took to prevent being raped, but the reality is that no one can predict how they would react until they're faced with that situation.

Finally, victims don't always behave the way you expect them to. The way you think they should. The way you think *you* would. This is so important for law enforcement, medical staff, and the friends and family of the victim to understand. Just because the victim isn't shaking and crying hysterically doesn't mean what she tells you isn't true. In some cases, the victim may laugh or giggle while recounting the incident. This is normal. The victim may exhibit a flat affect and talk about what happened to her in a detached, matter-of-fact tone. This is normal. The victim may not be able to provide an account of what happened in chronological order. She may be able to provide specific details about something that seems irrelevant to you but can't provide answers to "basic" questions about the incident. This is normal.

Even though I didn't have any specific training on how trauma affected the brain in 2005, I had interviewed enough rape victims to recognize that Amy was in no shape to sit down for a formal interview that day.

During my interview with Amy's roommate, Kara, she told me that she woke up to find a man in the doorway of her bedroom. She immediately grabbed a baseball bat she kept next to the bed, but the suspect got angry and told her he had a gun. She put the bat down, and the suspect approached her. He forced Kara to kneel next to her bed, and he began asking for money and about who else was in the house while pressing the gun against the back of her head. He eventually made her get up and forced her down the hallway into Amy's room. Kara described how the suspect tied her up along with Lauren using a cable from the wall. She said the suspect demanded six thousand dollars, but she had no idea why he thought they had that kind of money. Kara said she and Lauren were taken into the bathroom, where they began to undo their bindings. The suspect saw that the two women had begun to remove their bindings, so he tied them up with cords from a hairdryer, flat iron, and clothes iron. Throughout the ordeal, they prayed out loud while being forced to listen to their friend Amy's prolonged sexual assault.

Brad and I arranged to meet with Amy the following day for an in-depth interview. During the interview, Amy told us she woke to find Kara standing next to her bed with a strange look on her face. A man in a ski mask was standing behind her roommate, holding a gun. He ordered Amy out of bed and made the two women kneel on the floor next to the bed. He demanded money and asked where the phones were.

Amy's other roommate, Lauren, woke up after hearing the commotion. She tried to run downstairs to call 911 but was quickly captured by the suspect and brought back upstairs to the bedroom with her two friends. The suspect led the three women around the house looking for items of value and demanded they give him six thousand dollars. He tied up Amy's roommates with a computer cable, and when that didn't hold them, he used the cord from a hairdryer to bind them. He forced Amy to remove her clothing and then made her place pillowcases over Kara and Lauren's heads. The two roommates were eventually forced into the bathtub while the suspect sexually assaulted Amy in the bathroom and one of the bedrooms.

After the last sexual assault, the suspect ordered Amy to take a cold shower and brush her teeth. Despite the nightmare she was enduring, Amy had the presence of mind to wipe semen from her face onto the bathroom floor when the suspect was distracted. Once in the shower, Amy was told to wash her hair and brush her teeth. The suspect soaped up his gloved hand and attempted to wash away evidence from Amy's body. She waited in the shower for about ten minutes until she was sure the intruder was gone. She estimated the whole encounter lasted about two hours.

During the interview, Amy was able to provide a description of her attacker. He was a black male wearing a ski mask with eye holes and a mouth hole cut out. She could see enough of his skin around his eyes and mouth to tell he was black. He wore gloves and was armed with a dark-colored revolver. Amy also recalled that he smelled of cigarettes. She had no idea who he was, and neither did Amy's roommates.

Back at the house on Trafton, the green and white toothbrush was collected as evidence, along with a bath towel used by Amy to dry off after the forced attempt at evidence destruction. A Forensic Specialist lifted a perfect shoe impression from the hardwood floor inside one of the bedrooms and an identical impression from the wood deck at the rear of the house.

I submitted several items of evidence to the crime lab right away, including Amy's rape kit, the green and white toothbrush, and the towel collected from Amy's bedroom. When I spoke to the DNA Supervisor at the Crime Lab, he told me that my case sounded eerily similar to a home invasion rape that occurred in August in the town of Fircrest, just west of Tacoma.

Fircrest is a one-and-a-half-square-mile town situated between Tacoma and University Place with a population of less than 6,500. There's minimal crime and almost no violent crime. While Fircrest has its own police department, major crimes are investigated by the Pierce County Sheriff's Department.

In the early morning hours of August 31, 2005, 19-year-old Jada Simpson woke up to find a masked man in her bedroom, armed with a revolver. He told her not to cry, or he would kill her. He also told her he was there to rob her. Jada's mother heard her scream and came to investigate. The suspect hid, and Jada convinced her mother she had seen a spider. After her mother left the room, the unknown attacker asked where Jada's phone was. She lied and said it was in her mom's room. He took her driver's license from her wallet and told Jada he would remember her and that if she told the police, he would kill her family. The suspect ordered Jada to strip; then, he began to violently rape her while her brother slept in the next room.

During the prolonged assault, the suspect indicated he had been watching Jada by telling her he saw her taking pictures in her room earlier in the evening. At some point, the suspect forced Jada to swallow two red pills he pulled from his pocket, then he stuck the barrel of his gun in her mouth. When the masked intruder was done sexually assaulting Jada, he made her give him a kiss and walk him to the door before he left—as if, in his twisted mind, they were saying their goodbyes at the end of a date.

After the suspect fled, Jada ran to her mother's room and told her what had happened. She waited about twenty minutes before calling 911 out of fear that her rapist would return and kill her whole family. Fircrest Police Officers responded to the call. It appeared the suspect entered through an unlocked garage door, but nothing else was gleaned from the crime scene. Jada went to the hospital, where she underwent a sexual assault exam. Her rape kit was submitted to the crime lab for DNA testing.

Rush testing was requested for the evidence submitted from both the Tacoma and Fircrest assaults. In Amy's case, no DNA was found in her rape kit, but a male DNA profile was obtained from the green and white toothbrush she'd been ordered to brush her teeth with by the suspect. In Jada's case, a male DNA profile was obtained from a swab of her breast and a swab of her neck taken by the Sexual Assault Nurse Examiner at the hospital. The DNA profiles from both cases were from the same unknown male. The profile was uploaded into the state and national DNA database (CODIS) with no matches.

At this point, we knew we had a very dangerous rapist on the loose, but we had few clues to his identity. The media was aware of the two attacks, and law enforcement bulletins were distributed statewide by the Washington State Attorney General's Office Homicide Investigation Tracking System (HITS) Unit, notifying other agencies of the attacks in Pierce County. We received dozens of Crime Stoppers tips, none of which panned out.

Nineteen days after the attack on Trafton Street in Tacoma, I got a call from King County Sheriff's Department Detective Mary Lisa Priebe-Olson about a home invasion rape she was investigating in her jurisdiction. The MO sounded like the same guy from the statewide bulletin I'd issued. After speaking to Detective Priebe-Olson, I had no doubt it was the same guy—but he was becoming more brazen and more violent. In the King County case, the intruder entered the ground floor apartment through an unlocked kitchen window just before 2 AM. He terrorized the five victims inside the home for several hours.

The unknown black male intruder was armed with a black revolver with a brown handle and wore gloves and a dark knit ski mask. He confronted a young woman and her boyfriend in their bed first. When the male victim tried to get up, the intruder threw an unknown powder in his face, pushed him to the floor, and stomped on his head. He used duct tape to bind the male victim's hands and feet and put a pillowcase over his head. While this was occurring, the suspect asked the two victims who else was home. He asked them, "Where's the money?" and told them this was only a robbery. The suspect told the two victims that he knew they showered together earlier in the evening, indicating he'd been outside watching the apartment for some time.

The suspect went room to room, taking control of the other two males and female in the apartment. He used duct tape to secure the two additional males and placed a pillowcase over one of their heads. After securing the three male victims, the suspect forced the two females to help him search for money as he ransacked the place. He became angry and began punching and kicking the male victims. He struck them with the gun when he couldn't find any money.

After an unsuccessful search for cash, the suspect directed his attention to the females. He forced them to strip and sexually assaulted them repeatedly. He punched the females and put the gun in one of their mouths. After raping the females, the suspect forced them to perform sex acts on the male victims and then each other.

The suspect seemed to particularly dislike one of the males and sadistically assaulted him by burning him with a cigarette, ripping an earring from his ear, stabbing him with a fork in both thighs, and threatening to anally rape him with a floor lamp. Throughout the torturous event, the suspect berated the male victims for being unable to protect their women.

Eventually, the two female victims were ordered into the bathtub, where they were instructed to wash their mouths and bodies. He threatened to come back and kill them if they called the police. The suspect fled the scene with a bottle of lubricant he'd brought and over $800 cash. He left his roll of duct tape behind.

Nearly one hundred items of evidence were collected from the scene, including orange juice containers the suspect drank from, cigarette butts, shoe impressions from inside and outside the apartment, and the duct tape left by the suspect. Rape kits from the victims were collected at the hospital.

After the King County attack, the media frenzy ramped up. We created a task force that included Tacoma Police, Pierce County Sheriff, King County Sheriff, Washington State Patrol Crime Lab, Pierce, and King County Prosecutor's Office, and the Attorney General's Office HITS Unit. One of the detectives on the task force was King County Sheriff Detective Kathy Decker. This was my first time meeting her, but we would collaborate on many more cases as the years went on.

Detective Decker was a Man Tracker. This was the first time I'd heard the term, but I was instantly intrigued. A Man Tracker is trained to track humans by interpreting footwear impressions and changes to the ground, vegetation, and surrounding environment. Trackers identify a "sign" the same way hunters track their prey.

Detective Decker was brought in to help interpret the footwear impressions found at the Trafton house and the King County apartment. She was able to locate impressions from partial shoe prints on the linoleum floor inside the King County apartment and from the parking lot outside. From these impressions, she was able to track the suspect through the parking lot and locate where he'd been and where he likely parked his car. She was able to send the partial shoe impressions from the Trafton house and the King County apartment to the FBI and got back an ID for the shoe worn by the attacker in the King County case. The shoe was identified as a Nike Shox Ride2. The shoe worn by the suspect in the Trafton case was a different model Nike tennis shoe.

On Halloween morning, I got a call from one of my old

patrol partners. He'd been working graveyard the night before and told me about a home invasion in the Hilltop neighborhood that sounded like our guy. I reviewed the report when I got to the station and learned that a woman in her 60s called 911 after a man broke into her house on South Sprague. Apparently, this same woman reported a prowler twice that evening before the man broke in. In both of the previous calls, the responding officers found no prowler and left.

Finally, at about 2 AM, the suspect threw a landscaping brick through a window and then jumped through the broken glass into a bedroom where a young child slept. Once inside, the ski-masked suspect, armed with a gun, corralled the woman and her two young grandchildren. He led them through the house as if he were looking for someone. He didn't say anything to them before fleeing. The responding officers found that the exterior lights had been disabled, and the phone line had been cut.

A report titled "Robbery Attempt" was taken, and no detective callout was initiated. After reading the report, I was pretty confident our serial rapist had struck again. Brad Graham and I went out to interview the woman who'd been terrorized that morning. After interviewing her, we learned that she had a 20-year-old granddaughter who frequented her residence but wasn't home the morning of the attack. After seeing her photo, I noted a strong resemblance to the Fircrest victim. Now I felt certain—his intended target wasn't home.

As if Halloween hadn't started out bad enough, there was a second attack that morning in Tacoma. And just like the earlier attack on Sprague, the responding officers didn't connect it with the serial rape investigation. I don't remember how I found out about the second one, but I do recall getting into an argument with the officer who took the report that morning. When I asked why he didn't notify me (after all, we had notified Patrol, issued bulletins, we had a task force, this was all over the news, and people were scared), he said it wasn't related to my case. He determined it was a neighbor dispute over a stolen XBox.

Bullshit.

So, here's how the second attack that morning went down. At about 5 AM, an unknown black male entered a ground-floor condo located at North 16th and Pearl Street in Tacoma. After gaining access through an unlocked sliding door, the ski-masked suspect who was armed with a revolver confronted the two males and female who were asleep in their beds. He bound the males with duct tape and then duct-taped the female's eyes shut. He located the victims' cell phones and either broke or hid them while demanding money. He forced the female victim to strip and then told her to call her 17-year-old sister to come over.

Shortly after the sister arrived, the two male victims got loose from their bindings and jumped out the bathroom window. They ran to a neighboring unit to call 911. When the suspect figured out the two males had escaped, he fled with a pack of Marlboro Blue 72 cigarettes belonging to one of the male victims. The officers believed that the whole thing stemmed from a dispute over a stolen Xbox and titled the report "robbery."

Believe it or not, there was a third attack that took place on Halloween 2005.

This time, he struck in Des Moines, a small community in west King County about 20 miles north of Tacoma. Shortly before 10 PM, the suspect managed to slip inside a locked exterior door, which led to a common hallway inside an apartment complex. A twenty-four-year-old woman and her twelve-year-old brother had just returned home from a Halloween event at the South Center Mall in the city of Tukwila. About five minutes after they arrived home, they heard knocking on the outside door of the building but didn't see anyone when they looked out the window. After hearing more knocking, three of the family's children went out into the common hallway, thinking someone was playing a practical joke on them. Suddenly, a black male appeared wearing a black ski mask with eye holes cut out and gloves. He pointed a revolver at the twenty-year-old victim's head and forced her along with her siblings back inside their apartment. Once inside, the suspect threatened to kill the whole family if they called police or tried to get away.

The family of six was trapped inside the apartment—a set of adult parents, two young adult sisters, a twelve-year-old boy, and a toddler. The suspect collected and then hid the cell phones in the apartment and demanded money before using duct tape to bind each person. He separated the two sisters from the rest of the family and took them into a bedroom. After forcing them to give him cash, he made the twenty and twenty-four-year-old sisters remove their clothing before raping both of them repeatedly for hours. After the rapes, he forced the two women to shower, then made them get dressed. He bound the two women together with duct tape and left a pair of scissors with them, instructing them to wait ten minutes before they cut themselves free. He threatened to return and kill them all if they tried to get free earlier or call the police. The suspect left the apartment but returned about a minute later. He told them he was just testing them. After that, he left and did not return. The victims were terrified and waited nearly ten hours to report the attack after one of the victims told a co-worker what had happened.

By this point, the public was terrified. I was consumed with the case, and my anxiety seemed to ratchet up as the days went on—when would he strike next, and where? I was having trouble sleeping and thought about stashing a gun under my pillow. This guy was so brazen that it seemed no one was immune. My husband was heading off to Eastern Washington for a hunting trip, so

I told him to go to Home Depot and get wooden dowels for all the windows and doors before he left because clearly, the gated community and alarm system weren't good enough. Once the house was up to Fort Knox standards, I only felt the need to sleep with my gun on my nightstand—not under my pillow.

We believed the suspect was targeting his female victims at some common location, but we couldn't find any common locations visited or frequented by all of the victims. Most of the female victims were young and attractive, with light or olive skin and dark hair. Based on statements he made to several of the victims, we believed he did surveillance ahead of time. As a part of the follow-up investigation, Tacoma Police detectives were assigned to conduct neighborhood canvasses in the vicinity of the Fircrest and Trafton crime scenes. We also canvassed the Tacoma Mall, handing out Crime Stoppers flyers to all of the businesses. We knew from our interviews that one of our victims worked at the Tacoma Mall, and two others had been at the mall in the days before her attack. We believed there was a possibility that our rapist might have been identifying and selecting victims he'd seen there.

Tips were coming in, and we followed up on the ones that were workable. We collected DNA samples from some promising suspects, but none turned out to be a match to our man.

November 8, 2005, turned out to be the end of the road for our rapist. Sadly, he terrorized three more victims before he was stopped. Around 11 PM on November 7, 13-year-old Hannah Jones and her 15-year-old sister Tasha were in their bedroom when a black male wearing a ski mask entered the room.

The man pointed the gun at the frightened teens and demanded money. When they told him there was no money, he got angry. He took their cell phones and threatened to shoot them if they woke their mother, who was asleep on the living room couch. The man asked if the girls could call someone to bring them money.

He ordered the girls to strip, then sexually assaulted them both repeatedly. At some point, Hannah and Tasha's mother woke up and came into the bedroom. The suspect forced her back into the living room, where he tied her to a lamp with duct tape and a dog leash. He also duct-taped her eyes and mouth. The suspect forced Tasha to shower before he took some pills and then fell asleep. At about 5:30 AM, while the suspect slept, the girls freed their mother and fled to a friend's house, where they called 911.

Officers from the Federal Way Police Department responded and surrounded the apartment. Shortly after 7 AM, the suspect walked out onto the second-floor balcony bare-chested, wearing the ski mask and armed with the revolver. After being ordered to drop the weapon, the suspect ran back inside the apartment. A few minutes later, he hurled an unknown object from the balcony into the bushes. Officers attempted to shoot him with a taser, but it didn't work. Then the suspect jumped to the ground and attempted to flee on foot. He was shot in the arm by a Federal Way PD Officer and apprehended. The object he threw over the balcony turned out to be a black revolver with wood grips.

I got the call that morning and learned that a suspect had been arrested in Federal Way, a city just north of Tacoma in King County, after a home invasion rape that sounded identical to the string of rapes we were investigating. My Sergeant and I responded to the scene in order to get an update. Assignments related to the follow-up investigation were doled out to detectives from multiple agencies. At the hospital, the suspect gave a fake name. He was quickly identified via fingerprints as 26-year-old Anthony Casper Dias, and he lived only a few blocks from the King County home invasion rapes that occurred on October 28. Dias only had one conviction for driving while his license was suspended. He had no felony convictions.

Dias denied raping anyone, even though he had duct tape

stuck to his underwear, and he was literally caught red-handed. He claimed he was just lying in the bushes when he was arrested.

Turns out, Dias was married with two young kids. We served a search warrant at his house that evening. Inside, we found a treasure trove of evidence, including a device used to test phone lines, a dark knit ski mask, ammunition, gloves, duct tape, and a pack of Marlboro Blue 72 cigarettes, identical to the pack taken from the North 16th Halloween attack in Tacoma. All of the other cigarettes we found in the house were Kool brand. During a search of Dias's car, which was located in the parking lot of the apartment complex where he was arrested, we found an empty package for duct tape and a pair of gloves with the number 207 written on the palm. This was the victim's apartment number.

After his release from Harborview, Dias was booked into the Pierce County Jail for Rape First Degree, Kidnapping First Degree, and Burglary First Degree. A search warrant was served on Dias, and a saliva sample was collected for DNA testing. The DNA results were turned around by the WSP Crime Lab in record time, and Dias was a match to the DNA taken from Jada Simpson's breast and neck swabs in the Fircrest attack, the toothbrush collected from the Trafton scene, a cigarette butt collected at the King County scene and a Coke can and cigarette butt collected from the Des Moines scene.

During a visit with his wife at the jail, Dias was caught writing notes that he tore up after they were observed by a guard. The notes were confiscated and taped back together. They included the following statements:

"I did some things, I robbed (sic) people."

"Sometimes, I had to get mean."

"I never hit girls, but I made them give me everything all the money they had lots they sometimes would hold out never had sex they say rape, but they don't say anything about 7,000. I never took all the shit in the houses because if I ever got caught, they know there (sic) shit."

"I've been on X every day all day. That might have made me think of a way to do crazy stuff for the money."

After a failed suicide attempt in the jail, Anthony Dias went to trial in Pierce County. He was charged with twenty felony counts of Rape First Degree, Robbery First Degree, Burglary First Degree, and Kidnapping First Degree. Each of the 20 counts included a deadly weapon enhancement. He was never charged with the Halloween home invasion attack on Sprague Street in Tacoma due to a lack of physical evidence.

The trial began on January 28, 2008, and lasted eight grueling weeks. During my testimony on two separate occasions, I was able to help paint a picture of the horrifying string of events for the jury.

When I got the call that the jury had reached a verdict, I literally jumped up from my desk and hustled down to the courthouse. Brad and I were in the courtroom when the verdict was read. Guilty as charged on all counts. After the proceedings, Brad and I were standing in the courtroom when Dias's defense attorney walked up and shook our hands. He congratulated us on taking a very dangerous man off the streets. Dias was sentenced to 227 years to life in prison for the crimes he committed in Pierce County.

Anthony Dias was charged with nineteen felonies in King County. He pled guilty to six of those counts on September 19, 2008, and was sentenced to an additional thirty-six years in prison. In 2017, he died of natural causes at the age of 37 while serving his life sentence at the Washington State Penitentiary in Walla Walla.

Several years after Dias was sent to prison, Washington State Senator Jeannie Darnielle sponsored a bill that would require DNA collection at the time of arrest for felony crimes. She used Anthony Dias as an example, citing his arrest for vehicular assault on July 31, 2005—just weeks before he began his home invasion rape spree. Darnielle and some of Dias's victims argued that many of the attacks could have been prevented if his DNA had been collected at the time of his vehicular assault arrest in 2005. Perhaps law enforcement would have had a DNA match shortly after the Fircrest or Trafton attacks, thereby preventing Dias from continuing on to harm so many more people. Sadly, the bill didn't make much headway.

According to DNASAVES.ORG, thirty-one states require DNA collection at the time of arrest for felony crimes. It makes perfect sense to me. We already take photos and fingerprints at the time of arrest. In addition, full name, address, social security number, next of kin, and medical history are all collected at the time of booking. When someone is arrested for a felony, they are usually strip-searched as well. I have a hard time understanding how a cheek swab is more invasive than bending over and spreading your ass cheeks.

DNA is such a powerful tool for law enforcement. It's an equally powerful tool to prove the innocence of the wrongfully convicted. In criminal investigations, finding a foreign DNA profile is only helpful if it can be matched to a known offender. Otherwise, it's just random pairs of numbers.

This was one of my most memorable cases for several reasons. Anthony Dias was a brazen predator who attacked people in the place they should feel safe and secure—their homes. As a detective, it was my job to help catch him and put him away, but as a woman, his brutal crimes terrified me. Several years after Anthony Dias was tucked away in his cell, enjoying the hospitality of the Department of Corrections, I had a frightening encounter that provided me with even more insight into what it feels like to become prey.

Early one morning, I was fueling up my detective car—an unmarked Ford Taurus at the commercial gas pumps located on

South Tacoma Way, not far from the station. I was heading in early to work out at the gym located inside the PD before my shift. It was dark outside, and there was no traffic at that hour. As I stood in the empty lot at the rear of my car pumping gas, I noticed a white sedan slow down on South Tacoma Way as it passed the pumps. The car continued past, and I got back inside my vehicle while I waited for the tank to fill.

A few moments later, I saw the same white car pull slowly into the lot and stop at the pumps adjacent to me. I could see there were two males in the front and one or two more in the back seat. I immediately knew something was wrong. These guys had no business being there— and they weren't pumping gas. I looked out my window to see the two males in the front staring intently at me with a fixed gaze. They clearly had no idea I was a cop. I reached into the backseat and retrieved my duty weapon from my gym bag. After I had my gun in my lap, I tried to decide what to do next. Get out and confront them? Request backup? As I contemplated my options, the car pulled out of the lot and drove away. I'm sure they saw me pull something from the back seat—maybe they saw my gun.

When I got to the station, I ran the plate. The car was associated with a registered sex offender. I wrote up an information report and forwarded it to the county sex offender registry coordinator. After all, no crime had been committed.

I have no doubt the occupants of that car intended to harm me. I could feel it. I don't know if they planned to rob, rape, kidnap or kill me—possibly a combination thereof. Even though I knew this to be true, I thought about what I would have said to the responding officer if I'd called for backup.

"They were looking at me."

The best I had was a charge of mopery with intent to creep.

CHAPTER 9

4th of July

In May 2007, Ed and I took a trip to Mexico. At the airport, I found a book to read on my vacation. Instead of choosing something entertaining or uplifting, I picked a true crime story about two girls who went missing in Oregon and were later murdered by a man in their neighborhood—what can I say? It was hard to turn off my detective brain. When I got back to work after my vacation, I couldn't shake the feeling that something like that could happen in Tacoma.

Just two short months after reading about the missing girls in Oregon, I was called out to investigate the kidnapping of a 12-year-old girl in Tacoma.

It was July 4, 2007, and I was at home getting ready for bed when the phone rang around 10:30 PM. I was on call and not thrilled to see Sergeant Davidson's phone number on my caller ID. "Hey Linds, it's TD. We have a possible kidnapping of a 12-year-old girl up at 25th & J." Sgt. Davidson said a gray van might have been involved. As I headed into work that night, I had a strange feeling; this scenario seemed surreal and almost impossible. Of course, I knew that child abductions did occur, but up until that night, I had never been called to respond to one.

Several possible scenarios ran through my mind as I drove:

Perhaps the caller misunderstood what they saw. Maybe the girl was at a friend's house and forgot to check-in. Maybe she'll show up when we get there, and everything will be fine. I had experienced these situations in the past. In those incidents, the missing children were always found unharmed. They always came home. But this time, it was different.

The first officers on scene spoke to the family and searched the home for Zina. They notified their supervisor, and an AMBER Alert was requested along with a detective callout. Detectives arrived at the missing child's home and conducted interviews with family members. The interviews were difficult because the parents spoke mostly Ukrainian, so a couple of the older children in the home acted as translators.

Twelve-year-old Zina Linnik was described by her family as a slender girl with long blonde hair and brown eyes. She was one of eight siblings. The kids spent most of that hot July 4th day at home. Later in the evening, Zina and some of her brothers and sisters went to the end of their alley to watch fireworks at a neighbor's house. Zina returned home, leaving her siblings at the neighbor's house. Around 9:30 PM, Zina's dad asked her to round up her siblings and bring them home.

Shortly after Zina left the house, her dad heard a scream from the alley behind the house. He recognized it as Zina's voice and went outside to investigate. As Mr. Linnik walked through his backyard into the alley, he saw a gray van parked on the east side of the alley, just north of his house. He saw an Asian male, approximately 5'8, thin build, wearing a light-colored baseball cap and jeans, walk from the passenger side of the van to the driver's side, then get in and drive away northbound in the alley. Mr. Linnik didn't see or hear Zina at this point. He and some of the other children began looking around for Zina in the alley. One of her older siblings found one of Zina's pink flip-flops in the alley, just north of their home, in the same area the gray van had been parked. After searching the neighborhood for 10-15 minutes with no success, Zina's older sister called 911 and reported that Zina had been kidnapped by a Cambodian man driving a gray van. Zina's sister told the call taker that the van's license plate contained the numbers 1677 and then some letters. During an interview with the Linniks by the responding officers, Mr. Linnik indicated the license plate contained the numbers 1677 and maybe a B at the end.

Zina's family reported that she was a good kid. She was going into the 7th grade at Jason Lee Middle School. According to her family, Zina didn't have any boyfriends and didn't have a cell phone or internet access at home.

I got an update on my way in. I learned that Zina's siblings reported that there was an Asian male who drove a gray van and lived a few houses to the south on J street. This man was later identified as Dan Lo. Detectives made contact at Lo's residence and found that the van and Lo were not there. I headed to the station to begin drafting a search warrant for the van. I also started digging up any information I could find on Dan Lo.

Detectives interviewed Dan Lo's brother, who said he could point out the house where his brother was attending a party. Detectives pinged Lo's cell phone and determined he was still in the area. Believing the driver of the gray van was a known subject who was still close by, Sgt. Davidson decided to hold off on the AMBER Alert request.

Lo's brother was loaded into a police car and directed detectives to a house a few blocks away. Dan Lo's silver Toyota minivan was located in the driveway, unoccupied. When detectives knocked on the door of the house, people began scurrying around inside. It turned out that Dan Lo had received a phone call and took off before police arrived. A police K-9 was dispatched to the location to begin tracking when Lo gave up and surrendered to police. The house was searched, but Zina wasn't there.

During his interview at the station, Lo denied any involvement with Zina's abduction and provided an accounting of his activities that day. Lo said he ran because his brother told him the police were looking for him and he didn't know why. He consented to a search of his van, which had been impounded and towed to police headquarters. The search turned up no evidence linking him to the missing child. Dan Lo was given a polygraph a couple of days later and passed.

At about 4 AM, I was sitting in the conference room with Sgt. Davidson and Detectives Dave Devault, Gene Miller, and my part-ner, Brad Graham. Our best lead had just disintegrated. Detective Devault, the senior detective on the callout team, looked over at me and asked, "So *Lead Detective* Wade...what do we do next?" The next logical step was issuing the AMBER Alert.

The AMBER Alert program was implemented in Washington State in 2003 and this was the first time our department had ever issued one. At that time, only our Public Information Officer could issue an AMBER Alert. Even then, only a complete license plate could be displayed on the highway reader board signs. Since we didn't have a full plate, the highway signs would indicate an AMBER Alert was in progress and to tune in to local radio stations for details. A call was made, asking the Public Information Officer to issue the alert. We later learned he had taken a sleep aid after working the Tacoma Freedom Fair that day and fell back asleep. The AMBER Alert didn't go out until late morning.

Resources from all over the region were deployed, and events in the investigation began to happen in rapid succession. By the morning of July 5, several dozen search and rescue volunteers and search dogs began combing Zina's neighborhood. A mobile com-mand post was set up, and the media converged on the neighbor-hood. The FBI brought in more than forty special agents to assist in the investigation, including members of the Child Abduction Rapid Deployment Team (CARD) and the Behavioral Analysis Unit 3-Crimes Against Children (BAU-3). The National Center for Missing and Exploited Children (NCMEC) sent Team Adam consultants—retired law enforcement officers with expertise in the area of child abduction investigation who volunteer their time to assist in the event of a missing or abducted child. The TPD Emergency Operations Center was activated as well. All of my department's available detectives, and many patrol officers, were assigned to the case. Officers from outside agencies also assisted, bringing the number of law enforcement personnel assigned to the case to over 150 by the time the investigation was complete.

By the morning of July 5, the core team of detectives, including me, went home and got a couple of hours of sleep. By the early afternoon, we were back, running down leads and trying to get up to speed on what had been accomplished that morning.

We obtained a list of vehicles with the partial license plate of 1677 from the department of licensing. We also compiled a list of registered sex offenders living within a half-mile of Zina's house. This turned out to be forty sex offenders. The information from the two lists was assigned out to detectives and FBI Agents for follow-up. A massive neighborhood canvass began, and a tip line was activated. Leads were evaluated, assigned, and tracked using the FBI's lead management system. Operational briefings for investigators were held several times per day, and the investigation ran 24/7 for eight long days. This investigation would become one of the largest in the history of the Tacoma Police Department.

That evening, Brad and I re-interviewed Mr. Linnik. Zina had been gone for close to twenty-four hours by that point. Special Agent Marti Parker with the FBI CARD Team came with us. We also gained access to a Ukrainian interpreter through the FBI. We asked for more details about the van and the suspect. Mr. Linnik said the van had a square back with two clear back windows and a bumper that was the same color as the rest of the van. He said the numbers he recalled from the license plate were either 677 or 667, with a letter before and after the numbers. I asked Mr. Linnik to draw a picture of the van, which he did. We also showed him photos of a variety of van makes and models, hoping he could narrow down the make at least. The two types of vans that he felt looked the most like the van he saw were Toyota and Volkswagen vans.

By the afternoon of July 6, we still had no solid leads. I hunkered down at my computer and decided to see if I could dig up any useful information from our law enforcement database. I learned to do this back in 2004 when I worked my first serial rape case. I searched for reports that contained gray vans or any vehicles with a partial license plate of 677 or 667. I found two police reports that piqued my interest.

The first was a suspicious person report from March 2006 at Wright Park, which is less than two miles from the Linnik home. The subject of the report was an Asian male from Federal Way, driving a silver Toyota minivan. According to the report, the man was watching women in the park and behaving suspiciously. The second report was a vehicle prowl report from a Lowe's Home Improvement store two months earlier. The victim in the report was listed as a white male named Jacob Frye. Frye reported that his tools were stolen from his van when he was inside Lowe's. His van was listed in the report as a gray Chevy Astro Van, license# B17667B.

I printed out the two reports and turned them in at the Emergency Operations Center so they could be logged and assigned out for follow-up. At the time, I thought the report about the creeper in Wright Park was the more promising lead, so Brad and I took that one. We tracked down the owner of the van, who provided a solid alibi. We also located his van and found no sign of

Zina. Detective Stefanie Willrich and FBI Special Agent Ted Halla were assigned to follow up on the Jacob Frye lead.

That evening, several detectives, officers, and agents surrounded the house next door to Zina's residence. An FBI Agent and a TPD Officer made contact with the male resident earlier in the day during the neighborhood canvass and got a bad feeling about him. He was evasive and nervous during their canvass interview, and they were skeptical of his story. His demeanor gave investigators reason for concern, so bloodhounds were brought in. The dog handlers had been provided an item of Zina's clothing to use as a scent article for the dogs. Several dogs alerted on the house, indicating they detected Zina's scent. At that point, the occupants of the residence were not home, so we kicked in the door and searched for Zina. There was no sign of her.

As the day wore on, tips continued to come in, including sightings of Zina, but none of the tips were panning out. A psychic called in and provided several locations where they believed Zina could be found. Even though we in law enforcement have little faith in psychics, detectives were assigned to search the locations provided. No evidence of Zina was found at any of the sites. Those of us working the case were frustrated but determined to find Zina.

On July 7, polygraphs were administered to Zina's father and brother, as well as Dan Lo and Zina's next-door neighbor. They all passed. Detective Stefanie Willrich and Special Agent Ted Halla had been assigned to follow up on Jacob Frye, the victim of the vehicle prowl at Lowe's. After meeting with Frye, they learned that Frye had been driving the Astro Van on the day of the theft, but the van belonged to his former employer, Terapon Adhahn. Detective Willrich ran a background check on Adhahn and found that he was a 45-year-old Asian male who fit the physical description provided by Mr. Linnik. Adhahn was listed as a level 1 registered sex offender (least likely to re-offend), with a registration address in unincorporated Pierce County. Special Agent Halla and Detective Willrich attempted to contact Adhahn at his registered address but found that he didn't live there. They were able to get a cell phone number for Adhahn from Jacob Frye.

On the afternoon of July 8, detectives were tracking Adhahn's cell phone in an attempt to locate him. They tracked the phone up to the area of Tiger Mountain Summit, just off Highway 18 in King County. After only a few minutes, the phone left the summit area and headed back toward Pierce County. Eventually, the phone became stationary, and the location was narrowed down to about a mile radius in the area of 112th and Pacific Ave in Parkland, a suburb southeast of Tacoma. Adhahn's van was spotted in the 1200 block of 117th Street, backed into a carport at a residence. Surveillance was set up, but there were only two police cars in the area when the van was located—Detective Brad Graham and another detective were in one unmarked vehicle about a block from the house, and I was in my unmarked car a couple of blocks in the opposite direction. The license plate on the van was a switched plate, which came back registered to an Oldsmobile.

We were in the process of asking for more units to assist when Brad notified me over the radio that Adhahn had stepped out the front door and then went back inside the house. Brad thought Adhahn might have spotted the unmarked police car he was in. About a minute later, to my surprise, I saw an Asian male matching Adhahn's description casually walking down the street, right in front of my car. I had never seen him before, but I had no trouble identifying him from his driver's license photo. As he walked by, I could see he was on the phone.

I got on the radio and asked Brad if he'd seen Adhahn leave his house. He said, no, they hadn't seen any more movement. I advised Brad that he had just walked in front of my car and that he was on the phone. Now my adrenaline was pumping, and I had no idea what he was going to do next. I followed him in my car for a short distance, waiting for backup to reach my location. I figured Adhahn was going to bolt, but a foot chase would have been the worst-case scenario at that point—I was outside my jurisdiction and had no fucking idea where I was. Trying to call out street names and directions would have been a nightmare. Luckily, he didn't run as I pulled up behind him. I drew my weapon as I got out of my car and yelled for him to stop. He turned around and looked at me, and he could see that I was the POLICE even though I was dressed in jeans and a tee-shirt. I had my GLOCK in the low-ready position, and he could see my badge attached to my belt. I observed that he had one hand in his pants pocket, so I yelled, "POLICE! Show me your hands!" He complied, and I ordered him to walk back to my car and put his hands on the hood. As he did this, Brad and another detective arrived.

After patting him down for weapons, Brad and I identified ourselves as Tacoma Police Detectives and explained that we were investigating a missing little girl in Tacoma. I told him that we wanted to go back to his house and speak to him. He was clearly nervous but agreed to go back to the house with us.

We drove Adhahn back to the house and walked into the living room. The house was a small one-story that appeared to be undergoing renovations. There wasn't much in the way of furniture in the place, other than a queen-size mattress and box spring in one of the bedrooms. There were two kittens in a crate inside the bedroom, which was suspicious to me—he didn't strike me as an animal lover. I advised Adhahn of his rights, and he consented to a search of his house and van. Brad began interviewing him in the living room while I began doing what I do best—snooping around. I noticed that the kitchen floor was covered with tools that should have been in his van. When Brad asked out this, Adhahn said he took them out of his van every night because he didn't want them stolen.

During his interview with Brad, he said he had dinner at a family friend's house on July 4 and was home between 9-10 PM. He said he watched some TV, although he couldn't remember what he watched, talked on the phone with a friend about the fireworks, then went to bed. Adhahn reported that he works in construction. When he was asked about his activities earlier in the day, he said he drove a friend's vehicle up to Issaquah and Redmond to look at a couple of jobs, then came home. Adhahn was asked about the switched plates on his van. He said his plates were stolen six months earlier, and so he took the current plates off of an abandoned car and put them on his van. He was asked about his sex offender status, and he admitted to molesting his sister in 1990. He said most of his family no longer speaks to him. Adhahn said he didn't see the unmarked police cars outside his house but admitted that Jacob Frye told him the police asked about the van. When Brad asked him why he took off from his house after looking out the front door, he said he was being healthy. Adhahn also said his mom advised him that the police would want to talk to him because the paper reported that the person who took the little girl was an Asian male who drove a gray van. He denied any involvement with the kidnapping of Zina Linnik.

As the interview progressed, more detectives and FBI Agents began to converge on the house. I could see that Adhahn was becoming extremely nervous as his eyes darted around the room while he continuously clenched his jaw. Adhahn eventually invoked his right to an attorney, and the interview ended.

Brad and I drove Adhahn to the station while his house and van were secured. We put him in an interview room while we met with Sgt. Davidson to come up with a game plan. We had no evidence to link him to the abduction, but we believed he was a viable suspect. After a short time in the interview room, Adhahn began banging on the door. He then told Brad we were messing with his sleep schedule. He went on to say, "Book me or get me somewhere to lay down." The only thing we had to arrest him for was Failure to Register as a Sex Offender. Instead, we booked him into the ICE detention center on a VISA overstay violation.

We were anxious to conduct a more thorough search of Adhan's residence and vehicle, so I wrote a search warrant that was signed by a Pierce County Superior Court judge. The warrant was executed by the FBI Evidence Response Team, and they conducted the search and crime scene processing inside the house and van. The inside of the van was concerning. There were no rear seats. The interior was pretty much cleaned out, explaining the tools all over the kitchen floor. There were two large plywood boxes built into the cargo area of the van. While the one in the back was large enough to fit a 12-year-old inside, nothing obvious was found during the search that would link Adhahn to the abduction.

While the search of his residence was underway, detectives canvassed Adhahn's neighborhood to see if any of his neighbors might have something useful to say. While none reported seeing a little blonde girl at Adhahn's house, one resident reported seeing him jumping over fences in their backyard shortly before the police converged on his house that evening.

At this point in the investigation, we believed Adhahn was a very good suspect. He was a registered sex offender who matched the description provided by Zina's father. He drove a gray van, and his license plate contained the partial digits reported by Mr. Linnik. The switched license plate was a red flag that couldn't be ignored, and he had no credible alibi. While all of this information was suspicious—including hurdling backyard fences, we didn't have one piece of incontrovertible evidence against him.

The search of Adhahn's house and van turned up no trace of

the girl, and those of us working the case anticipated the worst.

In the following days, we dug deep into Adhahn's history, looking for anything that might lead us to Zina. Adhahn was working in construction at the time of this investigation but was formerly enlisted in the US ARMY and had been briefly stationed in south Pierce County at Fort Lewis in the late 1980s to early 1990s. He also worked as a tow truck driver in the past.

We obtained a list of his previously owned vehicles and found that he used to own a black 1996 Toyota pickup. Interviews were conducted with his known relatives and associates, and searches were conducted at all of the known properties where Adhahn previously did construction work. During the investigation, a 2004 Child Protective Services referral naming Adhahn was uncovered. The complainant said Adhahn was having sex with fifteen-year-old Lana Ngo and that Lana's mother sold her to Adhahn for sex. The referral had not been investigated previously.

FBI agents tracked down the victim from the referral, Lana Ngo, now an adult living out of state. Her interview painted a grim picture of what her life had been like when she lived with Adhahn. According to Lana, she was given to Adhahn by her mother when she was a teen. She had been living in Texas when her mother met Adhahn, and he brought her back to live with him in Tacoma around the year 2000. She reported that she was raped by Adhahn on a regular basis. Eventually, he threatened her with a gun, and she left to live with a friend.

As we gained a clearer picture of Terapon Adhahn, a couple of unsolved cases were explored in connection with him. In May of 2000, an eleven-year-old girl named Sarah Erickson was found walking along a road on Fort Lewis ARMY base. She had duct tape stuck to both wrists, and she was carrying a stick when a female soldier found her and called police.

Sarah reported that she was walking to school on the eastside of Tacoma when she was confronted by a man standing next to a black truck. The man said "hi," and as she walked past, he grabbed her and forced her into his truck. Once inside the truck, the man used duct tape to bind her wrists and to cover her eyes and mouth. He drove her to a remote training area on Fort Lewis Army Base, where he brutally sexually assaulted her and then left her in the woods still duct-taped and blindfolded. Remarkably, Sarah was able to find her way back to a main road and was picked up by the passing soldier.

At the hospital, surgery was required to repair Sarah's injuries from the rape. She gave police a description of her attacker and his truck. She said he was an Asian or Hispanic male with short dark hair that was flat on top. She described the truck as a full-size black pickup with an extended cab. Sarah was able to work with the Tacoma Police Department's talented sketch artist, Detective Steve Shake, to create a composite of the suspect.

Detectives located the crime scene and found unique tire tracks in the mud. Plaster casts of the tracks were made, and the tires were identified as TSL/Thornbird off-road tires.

A male DNA profile was obtained from evidence collected during Sarah's sexual assault exam. The DNA profile was entered into the state and national DNA database, but there were no matches. Detectives spent hundreds of hours investigating the case but were unable to identify the suspect. Deputy Prosecuting Attorney Mary Robnett kept a copy of the suspect composite pinned to the wall next to her desk—this horrific case stuck with her. In 2002, Mary filed charges against the unknown suspect, utilizing what's known as a John Doe warrant. Instead of a name on the warrant, the unknown suspect's DNA profile was listed. A John Doe warrant is a way to keep the statute of limitations from running out on a crime. Once the warrant is issued, the suspect can be charged with the crime once his identity becomes known, regardless of how many years have passed since the crime was committed.

The other case that piqued our interest was more recent. On December 2, 2005, 10-year-old Adre'anna Jackson left her house in Tillicum on foot, headed for Tillicum Elementary. The town of Tillicum is located adjacent to Ft Lewis Army Base. Unbeknownst to Adre'anna, school was canceled that day due to snow. She never made it back home. A massive search was conducted in the area between the 4th grader's home and school, but the search wasn't successful. Four months later, in April 2006, neighborhood boys playing in an overgrown lot about two miles from Adre'anna's home located her skeletal remains. No arrest was made, and the case remains unsolved.

On July 10, a massive search for Zina was conducted at the Tiger Mountain Summit. The summit is a well-traveled recreational spot for hikers and outdoor enthusiasts, with an extensive trail system through the wilderness. King County Search and Rescue organized the search, which included dogs and volunteers combing the heavily wooded trails and underbrush. While at the command post, I contacted the Washington State CODIS manager to inquire about whether or not Adhahn had a DNA profile in CODIS. I found out that even though he was a registered sex offender, his DNA had never been entered into CODIS, the national DNA database.

At one point during the day, a hiker called the tip line to say that she'd been hiking the summit recently and saw a fresh grave along a hiking trail. She was asked to return to the location and led a deputy to a wooded area and pointed out a mound of dirt with a shovel sticking out of it. Yep, it looked like a grave, alright.

I was stationed at the location while waiting for the FBI Evidence Response Team to respond. Did I mention this was a hot and humid mid-July day, with flying insects the size of small rodents? I was about to commandeer insect repellent when the

King County Homicide Sergeant stopped me and said bug spray could throw off time of death since it kills the flies too. Fantastic.

I called Brad, who was greeted with a string of expletives upon answering my call. It didn't get any better when I learned that he was seated in an air-conditioned car, scarfing burgers and fries from the legendary Seattle burger joint—Dick's, while on the way back from checking out a tip in Snohomish County. He tried to cheer me up by telling me his fries were cold. I wasn't amused. By this point, I was exhausted. The few hours I had slept each night were restless, and I had trouble shutting my brain off. The case was taking a toll on me.

Eventually, the Evidence Response Team arrived and donned moon suits. After several hours processing the scene, they excavated enough of the grave to determine that it contained a dead ferret.

In case you were wondering—that case is still unsolved.

For the next few days, my arms were covered in half-dollar-sized red welts from all the bug bites. By July 12, we had turned over every stone we could think of and still couldn't find Zina. We were frustrated and exhausted. We learned from FBI profilers that they had success with finding kidnapping victims in the past when the death penalty was taken off the table. We met with the Pierce County Prosecuting Attorney and his Deputy Prosecutors to discuss this idea. We briefed them on the circumstantial case we had built so far and explained that we had reason to believe Adhahn may be responsible for the 2000 kidnapping and rape of Sarah Erickson and that there was probable cause to charge Adhahn with multiple counts of rape for his long-term victim, Lana Ngo. We also explained that he was a person of interest in the 2005 murder of Adre'anna Jackson.

Prosecutor Horne agreed that he would not seek the death penalty if Adhahn would lead us to Zina. We then met with the head of the Pierce County Department of Assigned Counsel. We explained everything we had told Horne to the attorney. During the meeting, a detective called to tell us that he had just met with Adhahn's ex-girlfriend, and she provided him with a photo of Adhahn's black 1996 Toyota pickup truck. The photo clearly showed TSL/Thornbird tires on the truck—the same tires identified in the Sarah Erickson Attack. We related this new piece of the puzzle, and to his credit, the attorney wasted no time. He got up from his desk and drove straight to the ICE detention center to meet with Adhahn.

Brad and I followed the attorney in our car to the detention center, accompanied by a Deputy Prosecuting Attorney. We waited in a small room while the attorney met privately with Adhahn. It had been close to an hour when he emerged from the meeting. I searched his face for some sign that we were on the right track, but I got nothing. "He says he can't help you."

We were deflated. Before leaving, we talked to a guard and gave him our phone numbers. We asked him to let Adhahn make a phone call if he wanted to, and the guard agreed. We headed back to the station in silence.

I made my way back to my desk and dropped into my chair in a huff. I was reading through the voluminous stack of notes I had accumulated on the case when my phone rang. It was the attorney. He said that Adhahn called him and wanted to talk again. I jumped up from my chair and yelled to Brad, who was a few cubicles away, "He wants to talk!" As we made our way back to the ICE detention center for the second time that day, I was excited. What did he want to talk about? Had he changed his mind? I didn't want to get my hopes up again, but at the same time, I was praying he would spill his guts. We arrived at ICE in record time and waited with a deputy prosecutor while Adhahn spoke privately with the attorney.

I was practically shaking thanks to the high level of adrenaline coursing through my body. I don't think Brad and I spoke at all.

After what felt like a century, the attorney emerged from the interview room. He had a blank look on his face as he stepped out and said,

"He says he'll show you where she is if he can have a cigarette."

Up until that moment, we were not certain that we had the right guy. I remember thinking, *Oh…my… God, he really did it*.

"Is she alive?" I asked.

"He said she was gone when he left her," said the attorney.

As luck would have it, none of us smoked. Brad later remarked he would have shit a cigarette at that point if he could have. We managed to bum a cigarette from a guard, and in short order, we took Adhahn out to the yard to smoke while we devised a plan. Our chain of command was notified of the developments, and we decided to leave immediately so that Adhahn could lead us to Zina. We loaded him into that back seat of Brad's unmarked blue Impala. I sat next to him in the back seat while the attorney rode up front with Brad.

Several ICE agents, detectives, and FBI agents followed us as we made our way toward Eatonville. Adhahn directed Brad where to go, telling him the location was past the Eatonville Cut-off Road. As we drove, I could see that Adhahn was nervous, as he continuously clenched his jaw. I asked him if we would find Zina's clothing with her, and he responded by saying her clothes were on Tiger Mountain. At that point, the lawyer cut me off and said I could only ask questions about how to find Zina's body.

As we got closer to Eatonville, Adhahn said he was getting nervous and asked if he could have something to drink. We detoured our caravan along the side of Mountain Highway and sent someone into a stop-and-rob convenience store to fetch a Coke. While Adhahn smoked another cigarette and guzzled his Coke, I watched him closely, looking for any sign that he might try to back out and ask to be taken back to ICE. The pit-stop seemed to calm him down enough to get him back on track and ready to resume the trip.

We continued driving further into the country, where strip malls and gas stations were replaced by evergreens and scrub brush. The further we traveled, the more rural the surroundings became. Eventually, he directed us down a narrow country road near the Silver Lake recreation area. As the gravel crunched under our tires, I felt a sense of impending doom. The road was a single lane bordered by woods. As we traveled further, Adhahn pointed to an overgrown vacant lot with a metal chain across the entrance. He told us to walk onto the lot, and she would be found about twenty-five feet in on the right. Adhahn was left in the vehicle with the attorney and several ICE Agents. Brad and I, along with other detectives and FBI agents, made our way around the rusty metal chain and started looking for Zina.

It was a warm evening but still light out. The lot was overgrown with tall grass, weeds, and a smattering of wild daisies. Evidence of an old fire pit was found on the property. After a couple of minutes, an FBI Agent yelled, "I found her ."I walked over to a shaded area under a tree and saw Zina Linnik for the first time. She had been dumped like a piece of trash. I couldn't believe what I was looking at. I didn't say a word, just observed. I felt horrified inside, but I had a job to do. Like most cops, shutting down feelings of sadness was the norm and certainly necessary at times like this one.

Again, the FBI Evidence Response Team was summoned to process the crime scene. Eventually, Zina's body was transported to the Pierce County Medical Examiner's Office for an autopsy. I was still at the crime scene when the notification was made to Zina's parents. I can't even begin to imagine how painful that must have been for her family. The forensic pathologist who conducted the postmortem examination determined that Zina died from blunt force trauma to the head and asphyxiation. There was also evidence of sexual assault.

We obtained quite a few search warrants during this investigation. After the autopsy, we returned to Adhahn's house with another warrant to search for oranges since her stomach contents contained remnants of oranges or a similar fruit, and her family reported she hadn't eaten oranges at their home. When we arrived at the house, a detective noticed what looked like blood spatter on a wall. At the same time, I noted that the trash can in the carport looked to be in the same condition as the night we arrested Adhahn—full. As I began looking through the can, I found an empty roll of duct tape and a dildo wrapped in a paper towel.

We got another search warrant and began processing the house for a second time—this time with a TPD Forensics Specialist. A section of the wall was cut out, and the trash can was completely emptied and inventoried. In addition to the duct tape roll and dildo, we also found three zip ties that had been daisy-chained together and a package and receipt for a king-size bedsheet. There was no king-size bed in the house, and we never found the sheet.

We also got a search warrant for Adhahn's DNA. In record time (something like two days), we were notified by the Washington State Patrol Crime Lab that Adhahn's DNA matched the DNA from oral swabs collected from Zina at autopsy. The odds of the DNA belonging to someone other than Adhahn were one in 13 quadrillion. No other evidence collected from Adhahn's house or van linked him to Zina.

We also learned that Adhahn's DNA matched the unknown suspect DNA profile from the Sarah Erickson kidnapping and rape from 2000.

On July 23, Adhahn was charged with Aggravated First-Degree Murder, Kidnapping First Degree, and Rape First Degree for the crimes he committed against Zina Linnik. He was charged with

Kidnapping First Degree and three counts of Rape First Degree for Sarah Erickson. Additionally, he was charged with seven counts of rape for Lana Ngo and Failure to Register as a Sex Offender.

For several months, Adhahn played games with us, saying he was willing to submit to an interview, then changing his mind. On May 2, 2008, he pled guilty as charged on all counts and was sentenced to life without the possibility of parole.

On September 8, 2008, Brad and I accompanied FBI profiler Jennifer Eakin and her partner to the Washington State Penitentiary in Walla Walla for an interview with Adhahn. The interview lasted about six hours. Brad and I watched the interview from an adjacent room on video because Adhahn believed Brad and I tricked him, and he didn't like us.

During the interview, he explained what happened on the evening of July 4, 2007. He said he was mad at his ex-wife because he wanted to take his son to watch fireworks, but she didn't answer his calls and wasn't home when he showed up at her house unannounced. He said that he had been drinking beer and decided, "To hell with it. If I can't have my kid, somebody else isn't gonna have their kid neither." He said, "I wanted to destroy a human." He drove around the hilltop neighborhood, not far from his ex-wife's house, and saw Zina riding her bike. He followed her into her alley and turned his van around so that he could escape quickly. He exited the van and saw her walking her bike up to her back gate. He approached and said, "Hi, does this alley go all the way through?" She said she didn't know and turned her back on him to walk into her backyard. As she turned, Adhahn grabbed her in a bear hug from behind, covering her mouth with one hand. He said she screamed and fought him, but he was able to control her. He dragged her into the back of the van and then put tape on her mouth and wrists. He then drove around the corner and down the hill on J street to a business parking lot a few blocks away. There, he pulled over and re-secured Zina with zip ties. He then began the drive to his house in Parkland, which would have taken about fifteen minutes.

On the way, Adhahn said he could hear her chanting or praying in her language, so he reached down between the seats where she was lying on the floor and tried to tighten the zip tie around her head and mouth. After that, it was silent in the van. When he arrived home, he backed his van into the carport and opened the sliding side door. He said Zina was not moving and the zip tie that had been around her mouth was around her throat. He realized she was dead at that point. He claimed that he didn't kill her intentionally, but he recognized that no one would believe that. He said he carried her body into his house, where he sexually assaulted her. Afterward, he said he wrapped her body up in a blanket and left her in his laundry room for several days.

Eventually, he decided he needed to get rid of her, so he dumped her body near Silver Lake. He said he threw her clothes off the side of HWY 18 near Tiger Mountain Summit.

A few weeks after the interview, Brad and I took a drive out to Silver Lake. As we walked from the car into the tall grass where we found Zina, I was overcome with a profound sadness. The feeling hit me like a ton of bricks, and for once, I couldn't hold back my emotions. I tried to look straight ahead so that Brad wouldn't notice as the tears ran down my cheeks. When we got back into the car, he allowed me to do something completely outrageous and totally unexpected—cry.

As we drove away from that terrible place, I felt a deep kind of pain in my chest that I'd never experienced before or since. Despite the emptiness, I was comforted knowing that Brad was with me—and that he would never hold my momentary lapse into humanity against me.

There are still many unanswered questions from this

investigation. We worked with a very talented Analyst from the FBI Violent Criminal Apprehension Program (ViCAP) after the arrest. She came out to Washington for a week from Quantico and helped us build an extensive timeline on Adhahn that might connect him to other crimes around the country. So far, he has continued to deny any involvement with the death of Adre'anna Jackson, and he hasn't been linked to any other crimes.

It is difficult to describe the far-reaching effects of child abduction. Abductions are high-profile cases that have a devastating emotional impact on not only the victim's family but on the entire community. As detectives, we are under immense pressure to locate the child and apprehend the perpetrator as quickly as possible. The lessons I learned from this case will remain with me forever. There are images that I will never be able to erase from my memory, but there are also many extraordinary parts of the investigation that I'm proud to have been a part of.

Several years later, I was tasked with forming a Child Abduction Response Team (CART) within the Tacoma Police Department. CART is a multidisciplinary team made up of individuals from several agencies. Creating the team was a huge undertaking for the core group dedicated to making the CART a success, and the outcome was extremely rewarding.

In 2013, the Tacoma Police Department CART became the twentieth CART in the country and the first in Washington State certified by the US Department of Justice. As a part of the certification process, our team conducted a full-scale mock child abduction exercise. I invited Jennifer Bastian's mother, Pattie, to attend the event. While she was there, Pattie told Jennifer's story on camera for a video we made about the CART Team. In the video, she said, "Jennifer went around the Five Mile Drive…but she never came home." Years later, that statement is still chilling.

As a result of my work in the field of child abduction response,

I became an instructor for the AMBER Alert Training and Technical Assistance Program at Fox Valley Technical College, where I have had the opportunity to train hundreds of law enforcement personnel around the country on missing child and cold case investigations.

This was one of the most difficult cases of my career, *and* it was my first homicide as the lead detective. To say that it made a lasting impact on my life would be an understatement.

CHAPTER 10

Sex Offender Island

*I*t's 2011, and I'm at my desk, talking on the phone with someone from the Washington State Department of Corrections about one of my cold cases. Suddenly, it occurs to me to ask a simple question, "Do all of the Sexually Violent Predators on the island have DNA in CODIS?" On the other end of the line, I hear: "I think so...."

I transferred to the Homicide Unit in February 2008, shortly after the Zina Linnik investigation was over. I had one of the greatest detectives as my new Sergeant, Tom Davidson. Tom had been a top-notch investigator, working Sex Crimes and Homicide before promoting to Sergeant. As a former Marine Corps Drill Instructor, he could be tough; but he had a relaxed, personable demeanor that put people at ease. Tom and his talented, smooth-talking partner, Dan Davis, cracked one of Tacoma's most notorious cases—the Trang Dai Café Massacre.

On July 5, 1998, a group of Asian gang members donned masks, then stormed into the café and opened fire, killing four men and a woman and wounding five others. The investigation was difficult and complex, and witnesses were hard to come by. People were afraid to talk for fear of retribution by the gang. One suspect was arrested but committed suicide shortly after he was booked into jail. Another killed his brother and then himself in the parking lot of his attorney's office as detectives closed in to arrest them. Ultimately, six men were convicted for the mass slaying.

When I transferred to the Homicide Unit in 2008, I was the only female and only the third female detective in TPD history to be assigned to the Homicide Unit. I was the first female of color. Within a few months, Detectives Stefanie Willrich and Louise Nist, followed by Vickie Chittick, joined the team. As the minority, we ladies stuck together, and we did a damn good job. Most of the time, being a woman in a male-dominated field didn't faze me. Yes, trying to pee in a hurry is difficult, especially when you have to take off your gun belt and there's nowhere to put your pistol when you're on the toilet; the floor is not an option. But occasionally, something would happen, and I'd be reminded of how fragile the male ego could be.

One day I was at the range qualifying with my squad. I was the only woman in my group, and I ended up with the top score that day, which was unusual. I was a pretty decent shot—in fact, one of my classmates used to call me Annie Oakley in the academy, but I was rarely the top shooter. As I broke down my Glock at the cleaning bench, I overheard one of the male detectives talking to some of the others as they scanned the score sheet posted on the wall. "She's married to the Range Master…no wonder," he told the others. I had to laugh because this guy was clearly upset about being beaten by a girl. On a side note, Ed was in charge of the range at the time, but we never practiced shooting together. Not really my idea of date night.

Despite my occupation and environment, I refused to dress like a man. In patrol, it was mandatory with the uniform and all. But detectives wear civilian clothes. As a young officer, I felt the need to prove I was good enough to do the job. As I said earlier, females have to work twice as hard to be taken seriously in this business. I felt the same way as a new detective, but eventually, I knew my work spoke for itself, and I didn't feel the need to dress down in order to be taken seriously. My nails were usually painted a bold color, and my favorite work shoes were bright red patent leather flats, affectionately referred to as my Dorothy slippers by Detective Gene Miller. One day, a deputy prosecutor asked if I was sporting pink corduroy pants for breast cancer awareness. "No," I said, "I just like pink."

Working homicide cases isn't as glamorous as it looks on TV. For starters, I've yet to see a detective roll out to a crime scene in an Armani suit, and our Forensic Specialists and Technicians wear work boots, not Jimmy Choos. If you get assigned as the crime scene lead, you might be stationed there for anywhere from eight hours to multiple days, depending on the complexity of the scene. You often get stuck with smelly corpses in unpredictable and less than pristine locations. A lot of the houses I went into were not inhabitable due to filth. Bugs, accompanied by rodent droppings, were not unusual.

Another magical place was the medical examiner's office. You knew it was a bad day when you could smell the decaying bodies from the observation room. Every year I got closer to becoming a vegetarian. I suspect it had something to do with watching too many people being carved up like a Christmas ham. I remember one of the Forensic Pathologists remarking that the brain he had just dug out of some poor burn victim's head had the consistency of feta cheese. I no longer eat feta.

When I was newly pregnant with my daughter, Detective Gene Miller and I responded to a suicide inside a residence. The victim somehow turned a metal pipe into a gun and blew his brains out—literally. I remember walking into the bedroom, where pink gelatinous brain matter was dripping from the ceiling, and the Medical Examiner Investigator was scooping up the victim's eyeballs off the dresser. That was the moment I decided on two things—I definitely wore the wrong shoes that day (I had on my Dorothy slippers), and I would resign myself to desk duty for the remainder of my pregnancy.

During my time in Homicide, I was assigned Missing Persons for a few years. I also worked on cold cases in "my spare time."

On the evening of April 23, 1980, 19-year-old Susan Lowe decided to spend the evening at home watching the Seattle SuperSonics basketball game on television. Susan was an outgoing young woman who worked at a local furniture store. Susan's roommate, Donna, last saw Susan around 7 PM. When Donna returned home about 10:30 PM, she didn't notice anything out of the ordinary inside their apartment. She went to bed in her room as usual.

When Susan didn't wake for work the following morning, Donna attempted to rouse her. She found Susan lying on her side with the covers pulled up to her chin. When she couldn't wake Susan, Donna went to the neighboring apartment for help.

Bellevue Police were called at approximately 8 AM. Detectives determined that an unknown assailant had entered the apartment and attacked Susan. She had been sexually assaulted and strangled with her own pantyhose. A cutting-edge technique called iodine fuming was attempted by the medical examiner investigator to lift latent fingerprints from Susan's body with no success.

The next-door neighbors reported they had been home the previous evening. They were watching Charlie's Angels around 10 PM when they heard someone knock on Susan's door. The neighbors heard "a banging noise like something hitting a wall," then a running sound followed by a muffled scream. They didn't find this concerning and did not bother to check on Susan or call police.

Susan's case eventually went cold after the workable leads dried up. DNA testing in criminal investigations did not exist in 1980. It wasn't until 1985 that an English genetics researcher named Alec Jeffreys developed DNA profiling. DNA testing was first used in a criminal investigation in England in 1986, during the search for the man responsible for two child rape-homicides that occurred in 1983 and 1986. In those landmark cases, Colin Pitchfork was the first person to be convicted of murder based on DNA fingerprinting.

In 1997, Susan's case was assigned to Bellevue PD Detective Jerry Johnson. One of the first things he did was organize the case file. As with most cold cases, they often start out as a box full of miscellaneous documents, reports, photos, and notes. Old cases are usually handwritten or typed on a typewriter, with no way to index the information contained within the case. Detective Johnson took the time to create a name index so he could keep track of every person mentioned in a report and how they were related to the case. He made sure all of the evidence was still maintained and made a working copy of the case file, and placed the original into evidence. Other things that had to be done were making digital copies of interviews that had been recorded on cassette tapes and scanning the old 35 mm photos so they would be digitally accessible. Detective Johnson re-interviewed many of the witnesses and collected DNA reference samples from numerous persons of interest.

In 1999, Detective Johnson sent evidence from Susan's autopsy to a private DNA lab called Forensic Science Associates. The lab obtained a male DNA profile from the vaginal swabs using cutting-edge techniques for that time period. The profile was sent to the Washington State Patrol Crime Lab for entry into the state convicted offender database, but there was no match. In 2001, the Washington State Patrol Crime Lab re-examined evidence from Susan's autopsy and developed an enhanced DNA profile that was entered into both the state and national DNA database but again, there was no match. The unknown male DNA profile did not match any of the men evaluated as potential suspects in the case either.

In 2006, the King County Prosecutor's Office created a cold case unit, and Susan Lowe's case was the first case reviewed by the unit. Detective Johnson would work the case for 15 years before finally getting an answer to the questions he'd been asking for a decade and a half—who killed Susan Lowe?

Investigators rely on a belief that DNA can help solve cases ranging from burglary to rape to Homicide. A DNA profile can be developed from evidence collected from a person's body or from a crime scene. That unknown profile can be compared to a known suspect if the investigator has obtained a sample of the suspect's DNA. The other traditional method of identifying an unknown DNA profile from crime scene evidence is to enter that profile into the Combined DNA Index System (CODIS). All 50 states have their own CODIS database.

There is also a National DNA Index System (NDIS) maintained by the FBI. DNA profiles contained within the individual state DNA databases are regularly uploaded to the national DNA database. The National DNA Index System allows for comparison of Forensic samples with Offender samples in addition to other Forensic samples. Unfortunately, not all Forensic samples can be uploaded into the national database because the profile may not meet the requirements.

Since new samples are continuously added, the Forensic database and the Offender database are regularly searched against each other, looking for potential matches. In addition, the profiles within the Forensic database search against each other, helping to link multiple crimes even if a suspect has not been identified. When a match is made that provides an investigative lead, it's known as a "hit."

By now, you're probably wondering what I had to do with this case.

In June of 2011, during my investigation into a 1999 child abduction case, I contacted the Washington State Department of

Corrections about potential suspects within their system. This inquiry led to a conversation about the Special Commitment Center (SCC) on McNeil Island. During the conversation about my case, I casually asked if all of the residents at the Special Commitment Center had DNA in CODIS. The answer I got was, "I think so…."

The Washington State Community Protection Act was passed in 1990 as a result of several high-profile sexual crimes that outraged the public. The crimes included the horrific sexually motivated murders of three young boys committed by Westley Allan Dodd, the abduction, rape, and sexual mutilation of a young Tacoma boy by sexual predator Earl Shriner, and the abduction, rape, and murder of a young woman in Seattle carried out by a sexual offender on work release.

These brutal crimes prompted the legislature to pass the Community Protection Act. As a result of this law, Washington began requiring sex offenders to register once they were released into the community. The Community Protection Act increased sentencing guidelines for sex offenses and created the first law allowing for civil commitment of sexually violent predators in the country. In 2019, there were a total of twenty states with civil commitment laws.

The Special Commitment Center on McNeil Island houses offenders who have been found to be Sexually Violent Predators (SVPs). All offenders who have been civilly committed as SVPs have been previously charged or convicted of at least one sexually violent offense. In addition, the state must prove the SVP candidate suffers from a mental abnormality or personality disorder that makes them likely to commit predatory acts of sexual violence in the future. If these elements are proven at trial, the SVP is detained at the SCC indefinitely.

It is not easy to prove a person is a Sexually Violent Predator. There is an enormous amount of research that goes into building an SVP case. SVP candidates frequently have decades worth of sexually deviant criminal behavior in their histories that must be meticulously documented in order to prove the case.

Although most of the offenders at the SCC already had a DNA sample collected by DOC prior to their release from prison, I found out there were several dozen Sexually Violent Predators on the SCC roster who never had a DNA sample collected. Even more disturbing was the fact that nine of these offenders were deceased and never had a DNA sample collected.

I contacted the director of the SCC and voiced my concerns. He told me the policy at the SCC was to collect a DNA sample upon release from the SCC, not at the time of entry. The logic behind this policy centered on the idea that once an offender was locked up, his ability to further offend was eliminated, thus making his inclusion into the DNA database irrelevant. This kind of policy only focuses on future offenses but does not address the need to have DNA in CODIS for the invaluable purpose of solving cold cases.

I asked that DNA samples be collected from all of the residents immediately. After months of calling and emailing the SCC, I was getting nowhere, and I started to get pissed. It was clear to me that collecting DNA from the residents was not a priority. By now, you know that I'm not one to take no for an answer.

To remedy this problem, I contacted Assistant Attorney General Brooke Burbank in the Sexually Violent Predator Unit at the Washington State Attorney General's Office. I told Brooke about what was going on at the SCC, and she agreed to look into the problem. Waiting for results felt like an eternity, even though I knew that a project of this magnitude would take time. I felt like I was the only person who seemed to recognize or even give a damn that the DNA from the sexual predators at the Special Commitment Center could potentially solve cold cases. It took nearly two years and a ridiculous amount of persistence, but according to the SCC, all of the DNA samples were finally collected from the residents.

The Washington State CODIS Manager conducted further research and confirmed that four of the offenders on the original list had DNA profiles collected from other states, which were uploaded into the National DNA database. In total, more than three dozen new samples were collected from residents at the SCC. As for the nine residents who died prior to having a DNA sample collected, I was able to obtain bloodstain cards and tissue samples from autopsy for four of the deceased offenders, which were submitted to the Washington State Patrol CODIS Crime Lab. DNA profiles were generated for all four deceased offenders and have been uploaded to the Offender Index in CODIS.

As a result of this project, the SCC changed its DNA collection policy and has begun collecting DNA upon entry into the facility. All of the samples collected during this project were sent to the Washington State Patrol CODIS Laboratory for DNA testing and entry into CODIS.

Then, in May 2012, something amazing happened. Bellevue Police Detective Jerry Johnson was notified of a DNA match in CODIS linking a civilly committed sexually violent predator named Michael Halgren to the unsolved 1980 homicide of Susan Lowe. Michael Halgren had been detained at the Special Commitment Center twelve years earlier in 2000, and his DNA had never been collected until he was swabbed during my project at the SCC. When I found out about the hit, I was elated.

Turns out, Michael Halgren was working as a machinist in Bellevue back in 1980. He grew up three blocks from Susan Lowe's apartment, and his parents still lived in the same house. During an interview with Detective Johnson, Halgren said that he was engaged to his wife in 1980, and he would never have cheated on her. He said that he bought marijuana from someone who lived in the apartments across from Susan's complex. Halgren was shown a photo of Susan Lowe and said he had never met Susan and, of course, never had sex with her. When he was confronted with the DNA results, Halgren said he must have had a one-night stand with her but didn't remember it.

Halgren's criminal history was pretty frightening. He was convicted of Rape 1st Degree in 1989 after he abducted a woman walking to work in Bellevue. He forced her into his van and sexually assaulted her. A nearby police officer interrupted the crime, and Halgren was arrested. He later pled guilty and went to prison.

In 1995, Halgren picked up a sex worker in Seattle while posing as an undercover cop. Once the victim was inside his car, Halgren attempted to bind her wrists with zip ties. The victim jumped out of the car while it was moving, and as luck would have it, a Seattle Police Officer was in the area and witnessed the incident. After a short pursuit, Halgren was arrested and charged with unlawful imprisonment. He was sentenced to sixty months in prison. Instead of being released again, Halgren was detained at the Special Commitment Center after his sentence was up.

While he was at the SCC, Halgren admitted to raping more than twenty women after he was discharged from the Air Force in 1975. He also admitted to exposing himself over forty times and peeping in windows. According to the probable cause declaration in the Lowe case, Halgren told his female counselor at the Department of Corrections in 1991 that he had fantasies about stabbing, shooting, and strangling her.

It is pretty clear to me that the crimes Michael Halgren was arrested for are just the tip of the iceberg.

I was astounded by the news of the DNA match. My mission to get DNA from every resident at the SCC had actually paid off. Despite my excitement, I had hoped perhaps one of the sexual predators swabbed during the project would have been a match to the Jennifer Bastian & Michella Welch cases. Unfortunately, I had no such luck.

Detective Jerry Johnson was kind enough to let me tag along on January 9, 2013, when he arrested Michael Halgren at the SCC. Halgren was charged with murder in the first degree by the King County Prosecutor's Office. He eventually pled guilty to Murder 2nd Degree and was sentenced to 14 ½ years to life in prison.

Solving just one cold case is a monumental achievement. But how many states collect DNA when prisoners are released rather than when they are sentenced? How many other states have civilly committed sexual offenders who were convicted years or decades ago, before DNA was routinely collected? Do other states have sexual offenders with no DNA on file, housed in mental hospitals with no likelihood of ever being released? Answering these simple questions and closing DNA loopholes could solve an untold number of cold cases around the country.

CHAPTER 11

Bundy

" *What do you mean Ted Bundy's DNA isn't in CODIS?"*

As a detective, I had always been drawn to investigating crimes against the most vulnerable of victims—children. When I got the opportunity to begin working cold cases, I was intrigued by the oldest case on the books in Tacoma; the baffling abduction of Ann Marie Burr, an eight-year-old who'd been snatched from her bed in the middle of the night. I knew that many people suspected Ann may have been Ted Bundy's first victim, and I wondered if it would be possible after fifty years to solve the tantalizing mystery, especially since the case had been collecting dust for decades. As I learned more about the brazen kidnapping, I couldn't help but think back to the terrifying memory from my own childhood when I woke in the middle of the night to find a strange man at the foot of my bed.

Ann went missing from her family home located at 3009 North 14th Street in Tacoma on August 31, 1961. The two-story brick house was only a few blocks east of the University of Puget Sound; a private college Bundy later attended briefly. According to Donald and Beverly Burr, the children went to bed shortly after 8 PM, while Donald and Beverly retired at about 11 PM.

During the early morning hours of Ann's disappearance, there had been a storm that brought rain and wind. Ann and her 3-year-old sister, Mary, slept in their bedrooms upstairs while her siblings, 7-year-old Julie and 5-year-old Greg, slept in the basement. At some point during the night, Ann brought her younger sister, Mary, into their parents' bedroom because the cast on Mary's broken arm was bothering her. Ann was told to take Mary back to bed. Sometime later, Mary appeared at her parents' bedside again. When Mrs. Burr took Mary back to her bedroom, she noticed that Ann's bed was empty. After frantically checking the rest of the house, Mrs. Burr came to the horrifying conclusion that Ann was gone.

Beverly Burr discovered the front door standing open, and the living room window was also open. A white picnic bench from the back yard had been placed up against the west side of the house under the living room window, which was normally kept unlocked to allow access for the television antenna. This appeared to be the intruder's point of entry. The frantic Burrs called police at about 5:30 AM, and Tacoma Police Officers responded to the residence. The Burrs reported their cocker spaniel began barking at some point during the night, but they couldn't be sure what time that happened. No property was found to be missing from the residence, and it appeared that whoever took Ann walked right out the front door with the little blonde girl, clad only in her light blue floral nightgown. The Burr family's world would soon be turned upside down, and their lives would never be the same again.

The Burr home was scoured for clues, and several pieces of evidence were collected during the initial crime scene investigation, including the white bench, which had been examined for latent prints. A small partial palm print was identified on the bench, but it was not identified. Tacoma Police Detectives led the intense investigation into Ann's mysterious disappearance—neighbors were interviewed, tips were followed up, and suspects were polygraphed.

Incoming phone calls to the Burr residence were monitored by police, and known "sex perverts, child molesters and exhibitionists" were questioned (there was no such thing as a registered sex offender back then). Massive land and air searches were conducted throughout the neighborhood and surrounding area. Notwithstanding the massive effort, Ann Marie Burr was never found.

Based on what I'd learned, there had been a thorough investigation into Ann's abduction, but despite that fact, the suspect managed to slip into the silent home of a sleeping family undetected and escape without a trace. This crime was bold and extremely high risk. Was the kidnapper a skilled burglar or a neighborhood prowler with a propensity for window peeping? Since no property was taken from the Burr residence, and the crime occurred during the hours of darkness when people are expected to be home, it seems likely that the intruder climbed in through that window, looking to commit more than a burglary.

Ted Bundy was never identified as a suspect in Ann's abduction during the original investigation. Over a decade after Ann Marie's disappearance, Bundy was identified as a prolific serial killer and eventually captured in Florida in February 1978 after committing murders in Washington, Oregon, California, Utah, Idaho, Colorado, and Florida. Ted Bundy was executed at the Florida State Prison on January 24, 1989.

Ted Bundy grew up in Tacoma and attended school there. I contacted the Tacoma School District and verified that Bundy attended Hunt Middle School from 1960 to 1962 and attended Wilson High School from 1963 to 1965. No address information could be located for Bundy during the years that he attended Hunt Middle School, but a Tacoma School District employee who went to Hunt Middle School with Bundy recalled that he lived in the 600 block of North Skyline, near the Tacoma-Narrows Bridge. As it turns out, I walk by his old house on occasion when I'm heading to my neighborhood donut shop for a sugar fix. According to Pierce County real estate records, Bundy's parents, Louise & Johnnie Bundy, purchased a home located in the 3200 block of North 20th Street on September 3, 1965. The home on North 20th was sold by Louise Bundy in 2009. Ted Bundy became a person of interest in the Ann Marie Burr case based on his criminal history and the fact that he lived in north Tacoma at the time of her disappearance.

One afternoon in 2009, Detective Gene Miller got a call from the new owners of the home on North 20th Street. They had recently learned that the Bundy family lived in their new home and became suspicious when they found some unidentifiable burnt material in the attic. Of course, I jumped at the opportunity to check out Bundy's house. The house was an old craftsman that appeared to be mostly in original condition, including a creepy dirt floor basement and a dilapidated shed in the backyard. We retrieved the container from the attic and examined it with one of our Forensic Specialists but determined the suspicious item was nothing more than plant material.

In December 2010, I began researching Ted Bundy to find out whether or not his DNA had ever been collected and whether or not it had been entered into the national DNA Database. I started by checking with Jean Johnston, CODIS Manager at the Washington State Patrol Crime Lab in Seattle. Jean notified me that Ted Bundy's DNA was not in the Washington State CODIS database since he was never convicted of any crimes in Washington. I knew that he was executed in Florida, so I researched where the prison was located and contacted the District 8 Medical Examiner's Office in Bradford County, Florida.

I sent an email to an Investigator inquiring about whether the Bradford County Medical Examiner's Office still maintained any tissue samples from Ted Bundy's autopsy in 1989. In January 2011, I learned that blood was collected during the autopsy and sent to a private DNA lab, where an RFLP DNA profile was generated. Since RFLP is no longer the standard, this profile could not be uploaded into CODIS. In 2004 a request was made to update the profile using STR technology; however, there was not enough sample remaining to generate a complete STR profile.

Next, I contacted CODIS administrator David Coffman at the Florida Department of Law Enforcement. I asked about a DNA profile for Ted Bundy, and he told me that Bundy's DNA profile was not in CODIS and said that he had not had any luck locating a reference sample from Bundy that could be used to obtain a DNA profile suitable for entry into CODIS. He went on to tell me that he got calls from detectives a couple of times a year asking the same question.

During our conversation, I told Coffman that I would try to reach out to Ann Rule and see if she still had any of the letters Bundy sent to her from jail. Maybe we would get lucky and obtain a profile from the stamps. Coffman told me there's a Bundy museum in the FDLE Crime Lab and that the wax molds of Bundy's teeth that were taken during the Chi Omega Sorority murder investigation were on display there.

In February 2011, I contacted Snohomish County Cold Case Detective Jim Scharf. I knew that he was acquainted with author Ann Rule who wrote the book that inspired me to become a detective, The Stranger Beside Me. I remembered that Rule wrote about receiving letters from Ted Bundy while he was in prison. I thought there was a possibility that Bundy's DNA could be obtained from the stamps on the envelopes if they had been maintained by Rule. Detective Scharf contacted Ann Rule, and she confirmed that she did still have letters and envelopes from Bundy and that she would be willing to provide them to me in an attempt to obtain a DNA profile for Bundy and possibly resolve other cold cases.

About a week later, I had lunch with Detective Scharf and Ann

Rule at Anthony's HomePort in Des Moines. Meeting Ann Rule was such an honor, especially since her book inspired me to become a police detective. Rule provided me with a manila envelope containing three white envelopes, a handwritten letter from Ted Bundy dated October 26 (no year), and a copy of Bundy's fingerprint card taken in Florida at the time of his arrest. The three white envelopes were addressed by hand to Ann Rule's post office box in Des Moines, Washington. The return address reads:

T. Bundy
Fla. St. Prison
Box 747
Starke, Fla, 32091

The postmarks on the envelopes were from March 6, 1986 (Large 22 cent USA Flag stamp), August 5, 1986 (Large 22 cent LOVE Puppy Design stamp), and September 29, 1986 (22 cent USA Flag). All three stamps appeared to be the type from a roll that needed to be moistened before they will stick, not the newer self-adhesive type. Rule told me that she maintained the envelopes in a storage container inside of a safe at her home.

I contacted a Florida Department of Corrections Support Services Administrator by phone and inquired about the procedure used within the Florida State Prison regarding inmate mail. I was told that there is a commissary-type store within the prison called the canteen. Inmates can purchase stamps at this store and can also receive stamps in the mail from friends or relatives. When an inmate sends outgoing mail, the envelope is addressed by the inmate, and the stamp is affixed to the envelope by the inmate. The letter is placed into the envelope, and the envelope is not sealed. Personnel in the mailroom read the outgoing letters before sealing the envelopes and sending the mail out. The DOC administrator said as far as he knew, this procedure was the same in 1986 and that inmates have always had to supply their own stamps in order to send a letter. He recommended that I contact the Florida Department of Corrections Office of the Inspector General to verify the mail procedures in 1986.

I also reached out to an Institutional Inspector by phone who researched the inmate mail procedures and said that he could not find any written procedures on inmate mail from 1986, but said that he spoke with several staff members who had been working at the Florida State Prison for over 20 years and his understanding is that inmates have always had to provide their own stamps and attach them to their outgoing mail.

In June 2011, I got a call from David Coffman in Florida. He told me he was only able to obtain a partial DNA profile from the wax molds of Bundy's teeth. He had good news, though. He was able to track down a blood sample taken from Ted Bundy on March 17, 1978, after he was arrested in Pensacola, Florida. The sample was located at the Columbia County Clerk's Office and had been maintained along with other items of evidence from Bundy's trial. This was amazing news.

The blood sample was submitted to the FDLE Tallahassee Regional Lab on April 12, 2011. Coffman wasn't optimistic. The liquid blood was over 30 years old and had been putrefied. Thankfully, there was some dried blood on the inside of the vial lid that was able to be scraped off. Six days later, a full DNA profile for Ted Bundy was obtained from the crusty blood vial.

Coffman told me Bundy's DNA profile had been entered into the state of Florida's DNA database as a suspect sample. Based on the legal guidelines surrounding offender samples being uploaded to the national DNA database (NDIS), Bundy's sample did not meet the requirements since his blood sample was collected prior to his conviction and because he is not currently in custody.

I was incredulous. Ted Bundy didn't qualify for the national DNA database. Ted Bundy is the poster child for the national

DNA database. He was a cross-country serial killer who evaded capture because law enforcement had no way to connect him to the horrendous crimes he committed across numerous states.

Former Los Angeles Police Detective Pierce Brooks came up with the idea of using a computerized database to track serial murders nationwide because law enforcement had no way to communicate about similar crimes that occurred in different jurisdictions. Brooks investigated the "Lonely Hearts" murders in Los Angeles in the late 1950s. During that investigation, Detective Brooks had to resort to reading newspaper articles at the library to find cases outside of Los Angeles that could be related to his own. In 1983, he testified before Congress in favor of a new crime-fighting database that would be called the Violent Criminal Apprehension Program (ViCAP). During the hearing, Brooks used Ted Bundy as his example to demonstrate how a cross-country serial killer could have been stopped much sooner had the ViCAP system been in place in the early 1970s.

I told Coffman I wasn't happy about Bundy's DNA only residing in Florida's database since he was a suspect in unresolved murder cases across the country. As it stood, Bundy's DNA would only be run against evidence samples submitted in the state of Florida but would not be cross-referenced with crime scene samples uploaded by each of the other states into the national DNA database. Coffman also expressed his concerns about this issue. I suggested that he contact ViCAP and request that they send out a bulletin to law enforcement agencies around the country, specifically homicide investigators notifying them that Bundy's DNA profile was now on file with the Florida Department of Law Enforcement. Coffman advised he would make contact and also request that ViCAP notify the CODIS Administrators in all 50 states. I notified the Washington State Attorney General's Office Homicide Investigation Tracking System Unit (HITS), and they sent out a similar law enforcement bulletin in Washington State.

In August 2011, Gene Miller and I reviewed the evidence collected from the Burr home in 1961 and noted that scrapings had been taken from the living room window, which was the likely point of entry. A piece of wood with reddish staining was collected from the window ledge, and scrapings of a reddish substance were taken from the headboard of Ann's bed as well. I submitted the scrapings and wood fragment to the Washington State Patrol Crime Lab in an attempt to determine whether or not the items contained blood and, if they did, obtain a DNA profile. Sixteen days later, I got a report back from the lab indicating no blood was detected on the evidence submitted. The results were a huge letdown, but it wasn't all that surprising given the age of the evidence.

After several more months of legal wrangling, it was decided that Bundy's sample would be entered into the national DNA database under a category called "Legal." While his profile would not reside in the offender index, it would still be searched against the forensic index on a regular basis. Finally, in September 2011, Ted Bundy's DNA profile was uploaded to the National DNA Database. I was overjoyed—my persistence had finally paid off.

There have been no matches yet. Perhaps with the testing of thousands of rape kits nationwide, there could be a hit in the future. One major problem is that most law enforcement agencies don't have anyone working on their cold cases. Agencies around the country have evidence on their shelves going back several decades that has never been sent to a crime lab for DNA testing. Even evidence that was previously tested with negative results could be retested today using better forensic technology.

I'm proud of the part I played in getting Ted Bundy's DNA into CODIS. This was an important milestone in my career. Meeting Ann Rule was amazing, and investigating Ted Bundy myself was extremely gratifying. A few years later, I sat down with one of my professional idols—the original "Ted" detective, Bob Keppel. I grew up reading about Keppel and his work on not only the Bundy cases but on the Green River Killer and many more. I remember the day I pulled up outside Bob's house for our meeting. I brought a couple of his books with me, hoping he'd sign them, but decided that I didn't want to seem like a groupie, so I left them in the car. I never dreamed that I would sit across from him one day at his home to talk about Ted. That was a true honor.

A few years after Bundy's DNA finally went into CODIS, I met Mike McCann and Stephen Michaud. They interviewed Detective Gene Miller and me for a book they were working on about Bundy. Stephen Michaud and Hugh Aynesworth spent several months interviewing Bundy at the Florida State Prison after he was sentenced to die for the Chi Omega and Kimberly Leach murders.

During the early interviews, Bundy professed his innocence, but Michaud crafted a strategy whereby Bundy would speculate about the type of person who committed the crimes without directly admitting guilt. He ultimately provided vivid details about the crimes that would have only been known to the killer. *The Only Living Witness* and *Conversations with a Killer* chronicled Michaud and Aynesworth's many hours interviewing Bundy. As you might have guessed, I've read quite a bit about the infamous serial killer, and I believe these two books provide the deepest insight into the mind of Ted Bundy. On January 24, 2019—the 30th Anniversary of Bundy's execution, Netflix released *Conversations with a Killer: The Ted Bundy Tapes*, a four-part series based on Michaud and Aynesworth's books.

I believe the rapid advances in forensic science, coupled with the tenacity of those investigators who never give up, will reveal many more of Ted Bundy's secrets to the world.

I'm looking forward to that day.

CHAPTER 12

Mud Pit

I cautiously make my way down the dirt path in the woods adjacent to the mobile home park. I know it's going to be bad, but still,
I keep walking. I have a bit of a déjà vu moment as I walk under the
canopy of towering evergreens toward the site, knowing what I'll find.

I close my eyes and think back to that warm summer night sev-
en years earlier when I'd felt the same kind of impending doom in
the pit of my stomach as I approached Zina Linnik's lifeless body at
Silver Lake. I know I'm about to witness a display of pure evil, and
there's nothing I can do about it.

MONDAY 8/4/14

It started out like most Monday mornings. A stop at Starbucks,
followed by a short drive to the station. As I sipped my soy mocha
in the car, a news report grabbed my attention. A six-year-old girl
was missing from a neighboring jurisdiction—and although she
hadn't been seen since Saturday evening, a missing person report
hadn't been filed until Sunday night.

Something in my gut told me this wouldn't end well.

The date wasn't lost on me either—August 4 happened to be
the 28th anniversary of Jennifer Bastian's unsolved abduction and

murder in Tacoma's Point Defiance Park.

At the time, I was the assistant coordinator for the Tacoma Police Child Abduction Response Team (CART), and while we focused on incidents within the city of Tacoma, we also assisted other agencies when needed. I decided to call FBI Special Agent Kyle McNeal to find out what he knew.

Kyle was a member of the Tacoma Police CART, and I figured he might have some additional information about the case. I also knew it was standard practice for the FBI to offer assistance to any law enforcement agency investigating a possible child abduction. Kyle told me he didn't know anything about the missing six-year-old, but he would make some calls and get back to me.

In the early afternoon, Kyle called and requested I meet him at the Kitsap County Sheriff's Office Command Post, which had been set up at a Fire Station located at 7600 Old Military Rd in unincorporated Kitsap County. I alerted Lieutenant Rob Jepson, the Tacoma Police CART Commander, and we went to see if we could be of assistance.

The command post was located about forty miles west of Tacoma. After crossing over a strait within Puget Sound called the Narrows by way of the Tacoma-Narrows Bridge, the landscape began to look more rural the farther west we traveled—gangly Madrona trees with their red peeling bark were interspersed with majestic evergreens and saltwater inlets bordering the highway.

When Lieutenant Rob Jepson and I arrived, we met with Special Agent Kyle McNeal and two Kitsap County Sheriff's Office Lieutenants at the command post, which was basically a converted motorhome. A Kitsap County Senior Deputy Prosecuting Attorney arrived a short time later.

The fire station lot buzzed with activity—volunteer searchers waiting for assignments, deputies coming and going, and red cross volunteers setting up a feeding station. Phones rang, police radios crackled—there was an overwhelming sense of urgency to find the little girl.

The Criminal Investigations Lieutenant gave us the rundown—we learned the missing child was six-year-old Jenise Wright. As I studied a photo of the doe-eyed girl with shoulder-length raven hair and a huge toothy grin, I was reminded of the cartoon character, Dora the Explorer.

Jenise was reportedly last seen by her parents on the evening of Saturday, August 2, between 10 and 11 PM, when she went to bed. She wasn't reported missing until Sunday, August 3, just before 10 PM, after her siblings went looking for her in the mobile home park and couldn't find her. The call was made by Jenise's twelve-year-old sister after an unsuccessful attempt to locate her.

Jenise's father eventually spoke to the dispatcher and didn't sound overly concerned about his missing daughter—he believed she was likely at a friend's house within the neighborhood.

According to the family and neighbors, Jenise was a free-range kid who wandered around the trailer park regularly. The neighborhood was well kept and considered safe by its residents, with just over one hundred mobile homes making up the development. A wooded area frequented by the neighborhood kids bordered the trailer park. With only one vehicle access point into the neighborhood from the street, the community seemed fairly benign.

Once Kitsap County Sheriff's Deputies arrived, they began an investigation. Within a short period of time, a roadblock was set up at the entrance to the mobile home park. A Deputy asked anyone attempting to exit for permission to search their vehicle for the missing child.

Investigators were called out to the scene, and Detective Lissa Gundrum was assigned as the lead.

There were obvious questions that needed to be answered. Why had Jenise's parents waited nearly twenty-four hours to report her missing? In any child abduction investigation, police must conduct a multi-tiered investigation that focuses on the family, acquaintances, and the unlikely possibility that the child was abducted by a stranger. Based on the significant delay in reporting her missing, Jenise's family would have to be looked at closely. Believe it or not, child abductions are extremely rare. A study conducted by the Washington State Attorney General's Office in 2006 estimated that about one hundred child abduction murders occur annually in the United States.

Jenise's parents were being interviewed by detectives, and Search, and Rescue had been actively looking for Jenise since the early morning hours. We learned that an Endangered Missing Person Alert had been issued for Jenise by the Washington State Patrol. An AMBER Alert was not issued because the circumstances and facts known at the time didn't meet the criteria for an AMBER Alert. In order to issue an AMBER Alert, there must be a known abduction. In this case, we didn't have that. There was no eye-witness and no suspect vehicle description, and while we strongly believed something bad had happened to Jenise, there was no proof she'd been kidnapped.

The next piece of information I heard made my blood run cold. Search and Rescue volunteers located a pair of bloodstained children's underwear, size five, along with a pair of child-size black shorts, in the woods behind the mobile home park where Jenise lived. As I scrutinized a photo of the bloody underpants, I cringed. I could just as easily have been looking at a pair of my own daughter's underwear—she'd worn the same size at that time.

I contacted the National Center for Missing and Exploited Children and requested assistance from Team Adam, a group of retired detectives with expertise in the investigation of missing kids and crimes against children. In the event of a child abduction, these volunteers are available to deploy anywhere in the country.

It was clear that we were going to need all the help we could get to bring about a swift resolution to the case. Lieutenant Rob Jepson requested the assistance of additional Tacoma Police personnel, and two Tacoma Police Detectives were assigned to make contact with Jenise's mother at her mobile home. The detectives were provided with a photo of the underpants and shorts found in the woods, and after showing it to Jenise's mother, she positively identified the underwear as belonging to Jenise. Mrs. Wright wasn't certain about the shorts.

I helped to brief the canvass teams on the facts known at the time and gave instructions for conducting the neighborhood canvass in the mobile home park. Registered Sex Offenders living within two miles of the victim's residence were assigned to FBI agents for interviews as well.

As we got further into the evening with still no sign of Jenise, I decided to reach out to my old friend, Kathy Decker—Man Tracker extraordinaire. Kathy was a King County Sheriff's Detective with a unique skill as a human tracker. I gave her the rundown on what was happening and asked for her help in the search for Jenise. After receiving approval from her agency, Kathy agreed to respond to the command post the following morning, along with another tracker from the King County Sheriff's Department.

Additional personnel continued to arrive throughout the evening, and we quickly realized the motorhome wasn't cutting it. The fire department allowed us to take over their training classroom inside the fire station. FBI personnel funneled in and set up a tip line along with the ORION lead management system to track all incoming tips and leads. Based on standard protocol for child abduction investigations, the Washington State Patrol Crime Scene Response Team began processing Jenise's residence, looking for any evidence that might lead to her whereabouts.

I left the command post late that night but agreed to return in the morning to continue assisting any way I could. This would turn out to be an incredibly long and agonizing week. A week of leaving early and getting home late, and only catching a glimpse of my own daughter on her baby monitor as she slept. I couldn't help thinking of her as I worked the case. The thought of ever not knowing where she was—if she was hurt or scared—was horrifying. Despite missing my time with her, I was thankful she was safe, and I was all the more motivated to help find Jenise.

TUESDAY 8/5/14

First thing Tuesday morning, I headed out to the command post in East Bremerton, which was about sixty-five miles from my house. When I arrived that morning, I contacted a DNA Supervisor at the Washington State Patrol Crime Lab to discuss the case. She agreed to expedite the DNA analysis of the clothing and DNA reference samples provided by Jenise's parents and requested that they be brought to the Lab in Seattle as soon as possible.

The FBI put Jenise's parents up at a local motel since their home was being processed as a potential crime scene. A Victim Specialist with the FBI was assigned, along with a detective, to liaison with the family.

Lieutenant Rob Jepson assisted with establishing a command structure for the massive investigation utilizing the Tacoma Police CART protocol. An FBI agent and I were assigned to coordinate Lead Management and Intelligence. Additional resources arrived to assist in the investigation, including members of the FBI Child Abduction Rapid Deployment Team (CARD) and the FBI Behavioral Analysis Unit 3 (BAU3)—Crimes Against Children.

I began constructing a timeline of events related to Jenise's disappearance based on police reports, computer-aided dispatch entries, witness statements, and other available records. This information was used by FBI Intelligence Analysts to create a visual timeline of significant events.

Two Team Adam Consultants from the National Center for Missing and Exploited Children were assigned to assist with the investigation. Throughout the day, Search and Rescue personnel continued to scour the woods adjacent to the trailer park where Jenise lived.

King County Man Tracker Kathy Decker and her partner located an area of interest in the woods behind the mobile home park that was in close proximity to where the bloodstained underwear and shorts were located the previous day.

They'd located a rotted fallen tree that caught their attention. In the space between the tree and the ground, they saw an area of compression in the dirt consistent with the size and shape of a small child's body.

While the man trackers' observations were certainly interesting, they didn't bring us any closer to finding Jenise. As the day progressed, incoming tips were prioritized by FBI personnel and assigned out to FBI agents and detectives for follow-up. Detectives from numerous jurisdictions arrived to assist with canvassing and lead follow-up.

By that evening, there were no promising leads and still no sign of Jenise.

WEDNESDAY 8/6/14

Wednesday morning, I was back at the command post for the briefing. I continued working on the timeline and also did some background work on financial transactions made by the Wright family. At about 3 PM, I learned that the DNA results had come back on the underwear and shorts found in the woods. Testing determined that the blood on the shorts came from the offspring of Jenise's parents. An unknown male DNA profile was also developed from semen on the underwear. The DNA profile did not match Jenise's father, and there were no matches in the state or national DNA databases. This was bad.

The identification of semen on the six-year-old's bloodstained underpants painted a horrifying picture of what might have happened to Jenise. She had certainly been sexually assaulted and injured. But where was she? Who did it? And why?

Once it was determined that an unknown DNA profile had been developed from Jenise's underwear, a DNA canvass was initiated at the Steele Creek mobile home park. I provided copies of the Tacoma Police Department DNA collection Consent form for the canvass teams, and they set out to collect cheek swabs from everyone who lived in the trailer park.

That same evening, the FBI flew in specialized K9 search dogs to continue the search for Jenise. Interviews were conducted with persons of interest in the neighborhood, and leads continued to be followed up.

THURSDAY 8/7/14

By the time I arrived at the command post Thursday morning, I was ready for a caffeine IV. It wasn't until I caught a glimpse of myself in the bathroom mirror that I realized I'd forgotten to put on makeup. That might sound trivial (and it probably is), but I *never* went to work without at least a little concealer under my eyes to cover up the bags and dark circles the job had permanently etched into my face.

DNA reference samples had been collected from dozens of men in the trailer park, and they were submitted to the Crime Lab for priority testing. Due to the seriousness of the crime, these DNA samples were being turned around in a day, which was lightning speed compared to the standard six to nine-month turnaround for most DNA submissions to the Lab.

Several men in the trailer park seemed suspicious for one reason or another. One resident left the neighborhood in a U-HAUL truck around the time Jenise was last seen alive. FBI Agents were assigned to locate the U-HAUL and process it for evidence. Another refused to allow his vehicle to be searched during the initial roadblock the night Jenise was reported missing.

The FBI K9 searches resumed, and the DNA canvass at the mobile home park continued.

Another detective from Tacoma PD and I began running background checks on the males that had been entered into the leads database as a part of the investigation. The names were from tips and from persons contacted or mentioned on the canvass forms. A canvass was also initiated in the neighborhood next to the mobile home park.

Around 11 AM, we got the tragic news that Jenise's body had been located in the woods by the FBI K9 team. It was a somber moment for everyone working on the case. While I felt tremendous sadness, I had a job to do—and that job was to find the person who'd killed Jenise and to help build a solid case for the prosecution.

I headed out to the body recovery site with several FBI agents, knowing it was going to be bad. The location was within the wooded area adjacent to the mobile home park. I had a bit of a déjà vu moment as I walked under the canopy of towering evergreens toward the site, knowing what I would find. I thought back to that warm summer night seven years earlier, when I'd felt the same kind of impending doom in the pit of my stomach as I approached Zina Linnik's lifeless body at Silver Lake. I was about to witness a display of pure evil, and there would be nothing I could do about it.

When we reached the spot, I saw her tiny body, partially submerged in a muddy bog. Apparently, the killer had placed a wooden pallet over the top of Jenise, which camouflaged her body from the searchers who'd been through the area previously. Jenise's body was in close proximity to the spot where her underwear and the shorts had been recovered, and the area of disturbance identified by Man Tracker Kathy Decker.

That same day, investigators attempted to contact seventeen-year-old resident Gabriel Gaeta at home in the mobile home park, but his mother said he was too distraught for an interview. She reported that Gabriel was curled up in bed in the fetal position and wasn't communicating. She asked that the investigators return another time. This seemed odd—other neighborhood residents had been cooperative. Was he hiding something, or was he genuinely upset about the murder of the little girl?

FRIDAY 8/8/14

With close to four hundred law enforcement and support agency personnel working the case, we had grown out of the fire station and took up residence at a local junior high school. The investigation had shifted from the search for a missing child to the hunt for a killer.

After the morning briefing, I continued running criminal history checks on the males entered into the leads database. I also requested a list of all registered sex offenders in Ktitsap County with no DNA in CODIS. After receiving a list containing eleven names, I provided it to the investigative support person managing the sex offender investigations.

The DNA collections at the trailer park were still underway, and the crime lab was still processing the reference samples that had been collected in record time. Investigators knocked on the Gaeta family's door again. This time, they got a sample of DNA from Gabriel.

That afternoon, I attended a briefing on Jenise's autopsy results from one of the attending FBI agents. The medical examiner determined that Jenise had been sexually assaulted. She suffered blunt force trauma to her head, and she'd been strangled.

On my drive home that night, I tried to focus on something else, but I couldn't help thinking about what Jenise's last moments must have been like. Hell on earth, no doubt.

SATURDAY 8/9/14

As much as I hated to do it, I took Saturday off to attend my niece's wedding. I couldn't completely let go of the case, though, so I took my work phone with me in the event anything came up. On the way to the wedding, I received a phone message advising that there had been a DNA match between a resident of the mobile home park and the unknown male DNA profile from Jenise's underwear. The suspect was identified as seventeen-year-old Gabriel Gaeta. This news was a welcome relief.

After the DNA match was obtained, two hundred and fifteen-pound Gabriel Gaeta was arrested at his home without incident. A search of his bedroom revealed clothing stained with blood and mud. An interview was conducted after the arrest by Kitsap County Detectives, and while Gabriel never admitted what he did to Jenise, he did say no one else was involved. He was a high school wrestling star and, as it turns out, a friend of the Wright family.

Investigators found news footage of Gabriel at a local vigil for Jenise, and his mother was interviewed by a local news station during the search. During that interview, Gabriel was seated next to his mother in the front seat of their vehicle.

What drove him to rape and murder a helpless little girl? I'm not sure I'll ever know the answer to that question.

Gabriel Gaeta eventually pled guilty to Aggravated First Degree

Murder and Rape of a Child in the First Degree. In June 2018, he was sentenced to forty years to life in prison for his crimes.

I learned some valuable lessons during this intense, multifaceted investigation. With close to four hundred law enforcement and support personnel involved in this investigation, it was certainly one of the largest cases I worked on.

It would have been easy to get tunnel vision from the start and focus on the victim's family for obvious reasons. But guess what? Despite their delay in reporting—coupled with their lack of outward hysteria—they had nothing to do with the disappearance of their daughter.

The killer turned out to be a kid himself who blended into the background, all the while hiding in plain sight.

CHAPTER 13

Untested Rape Kits

We're seated in a cramped office inside the prison. I slide a color crime scene photograph across the old battered desk so that it's in front of him. He studies the image of a white milky liquid left in the alley on Yakima Avenue.

"Do you know what that is?" I ask.

"Semen," he says.

"Do you know who it belongs to?"

He looks up at me and asks, "Is it mine?"

In 2012, Detective Gene Miller applied for a federal grant from the National Institute of Justice called Solving Cold Cases with DNA. The grant allowed us to review unsolved homicides to determine whether or not they had the potential to be solved with DNA testing. We also decided to look at sexual assault cases that would qualify under the grant, which meant the case had to be a stranger assault with a high probability of being the work of a serial offender—or cases that could potentially be linked to homicides. Detective Brad Graham and I reviewed dozens of rape cases where the rape kit had never been tested and ended up submitting about 30 cases to a private lab for DNA testing under the grant. During the case review process, I was always looking for cases with similarities to the 1986 unsolved murders of Michella

Welch and Jennifer Bastian. I believed it was highly likely there were other cases out there that could connect the dots and that we just hadn't found them yet. Sometimes the location of the crime would pique my interest; other times, the MO or victim profile would grab my attention.

One of the cases I found during the initial review gave me pause—not because I found it to be all that similar to Jennifer's case, but because the victim was a young girl and the crime was so bold.

On a warm summer evening in 2000, nine-year-old Shana Parker was out exploring her Parkland neighborhood. She came across a stray dog, and like any curious child, she followed it. Soon, she lost sight of the elusive canine. Shana spoke to a man outside the Parkland Care Center who told her he'd seen where the dog went. He offered to point out where the dog and her puppies were bedded down. Shana followed the stranger to a field. When they arrived, he told Shana to walk behind an uprooted tree stump, and she would find the mother and her pups. Instead of finding what she was looking for, Shana was attacked by the man. He brutally raped her and then left.

Shana walked home and told her mother what had happened. The Pierce County Sheriff's Department was notified and responded. Shana was taken to the hospital for a forensic medical exam, and a detective was later assigned the case. He canvassed the neighborhood and identified a possible suspect after interviewing residents at the Parkland Care Center. One man identified Antonio Nieves in a photo montage and said he witnessed Nieves agree to help a little girl find some puppies on the day of the incident.

The detective showed Shana a photo lineup that included a photo of Antonio Nieves, but Shana did not pick Nieves from the lineup. No arrest was made, and the case appeared to be unsolved.

I called the Washington State Patrol Crime Lab and inquired

about whether or not Shana's rape kit was ever submitted for DNA testing. I learned that it had been tested back in 2000, and according to the report, a male DNA profile was obtained from the rape kit. The report also stated a DNA reference sample should be collected from the listed suspect, Antonio Nieves, for comparison to the DNA profile from the rape kit.

I was told there was a match in the DNA database between the DNA profile from Shana's rape kit and Antonio Nieves eight years later in 2008. This match was classified as a Conviction Match and was not reported to the Pierce County Sheriff's Department as a CODIS Hit. I requested a copy of the lab report and read it over.

I was confused.

I asked for an explanation of what Conviction Match meant. I learned this is a term used by the crime lab when an offender provides a DNA sample to the DNA database as a result of a conviction. Often, there is a match between that offender's DNA and evidence from the crime he or she was already convicted of. Because of this, these matches are not reported to law enforcement.

After hearing this, I looked up Anthony Nieves in our criminal database and, to my surprise, found that he was never arrested, charged, or convicted for any crime related to the rape of Shana Parker in 2000. His DNA had been collected in 2008 as a result of an unrelated felony conviction. When I broke this news to the crime lab supervisor, he was stunned. The match between Nieves's DNA and the evidence from Shana Parker's rape kit had never been reported to the Pierce County Sheriff's Department. At the same time, it appeared the Sheriff's Department never provided the crime lab with a DNA reference sample from Nieves to compare to the DNA from Shana's rape kit back in 2000. This case was a perfect storm of missed opportunities.

After wrapping my head around all of this startling information, I called Cold Case Detective Tim Kobel with the Sheriff's

Department and ran down the story for him. He, too, was disturbed by the strange path this case had taken. He reopened the investigation and, in short order, introduced Mr. Nieves to his new home at the Pierce County Jail.

Thirteen years after the crime was committed, on November 19, 2013, thirty-year-old Antonio Nieves was charged with Child Rape First Degree. He pled guilty as charged in 2015 and received a twenty-year prison sentence.

The Nieves case was certainly bizarre, and while testing the rape kit did not immediately solve the case—a fresh set of eyes allowed Shana Parker to finally get justice.

2013 proved to be a fruitful year for cold case investigations. After waiting a few months for results on the rape cases Brad and I had submitted under the DNA grant, I started getting lab reports. I got two CODIS hits linked to the same man. It was a name I knew well—Andre Taylor.

Both DNA hits linked Taylor to stranger rapes that occurred ten years earlier in Tacoma. The first case took place in McKinley Park. You remember that park, right? Donald Schneider terrorized at least one of his victims in that very same park.

In the early morning hours of July 19, 2003, Tacoma Police Officers responded to the area of McKinley Park after neighbors called 911 to report a woman screaming in the street. When officers arrived, they found the victim, Marci Bennet, lying in the street with a blanket covering her body. Paramedics were tending to the woman, clad only in a shirt and underwear. She was crying and had leaves tangled in her dark hair.

At the hospital, she told an officer that she'd been picked up by an unknown black male in the area of the Arco station on Puyallup Avenue. The man offered her a ride, and she accepted. The man drove to McKinley Park. Marci said she didn't have a clear recollection of what happened next. She did recall being on her stomach as the suspect tried to sexually assault her from behind. When she cried and screamed, he threatened to get a gun from the car. Marci remembered being hit over the head several times. She couldn't remember much more about the incident. A sexual assault exam was performed at the hospital, and a rape kit was collected as evidence. The case was not assigned for follow-up investigation in 2003.

The second case that hit to Andre Taylor occurred four months later, on November 19, 2003. Shortly after 7 PM, Tacoma Police officers responded to a reported rape in an alley in the 2500 block of South Yakima Avenue. Upon arrival, they found a hysterical 41-year-old woman named Samantha Carmen. Samantha told officers she was headed to visit a friend when a man approached her on foot and asked if she wanted to make some money. She ignored him and continued to her friend's house. As she headed to the back of the house toward the alley, the same man grabbed her by the neck from behind. He told her he would choke her out if she screamed. He dragged Samantha into the alley near an old green truck and undid her pants. The suspect raped her while they were on the ground. Samantha believed he would rob her, so she removed two rings and gave them to the suspect. After he was finished, the suspect fled north in the alley on foot. Despite a K-9 track, the rapist wasn't located.

Samantha was taken to the hospital, but she left before having an exam. Ten years later, she would tell me she left because she felt the responding officer didn't believe her story and because she was left in a room alone for a long period of time with no explanation about what was going to happen at the hospital. Overall, she felt she was treated badly and decided she'd had enough. She walked home alone.

Thankfully, a Tacoma Police Forensic Technician collected a sample of semen from the alley; presumably deposited by the unknown suspect. In 2003, the case was assigned to Detective Brad Graham for follow-up; however, Samantha did not respond to phone messages and could not be located, so the case never moved forward. At that time, evidence from rape cases typically wasn't tested unless there was a cooperative victim. Ten years later, the semen swabbed from the alley turned out to match a serial rapist named Andre Taylor.

I wasn't all that surprised to see Taylor's name on two DNA hits. I knew from an investigation the previous year that he was a very dangerous predator.

On the morning of February 20, 2012, I was at my desk, Starbucks in hand, when I read about a disturbing incident that had occurred three days earlier. I decided to dig into our report database to see if I could come up with a lead for Detective Ryan Larsen, who'd been assigned the case on his day off and didn't know about the incident yet.

Just before 5 AM on February 17, 23-year-old Susan Li was walking home from a graveyard shift at a local fast-food restaurant when she noticed a 1990's blue Chevy truck following her on 72nd Street. The truck passed her several times and parked along the side of 72nd street a couple of times to watch her. The truck eventually followed Susan through the Goodwill parking lot at 72nd & Portland Avenue and hit her from behind.

After the truck ran Susan down, the unknown black male driver exited the truck and attempted to pick her up off the ground. The commotion attracted a passerby who stopped to intervene, and the suspect drove away.

Susan called 911 from her cell phone and provided several variations of a partial license plate to responding officers, including 132, 104N, and 10N. The suspect was described as a dark-skinned male with a skinny build.

Susan sustained significant injuries and was transported to St.

Joseph Hospital and then to Tacoma General Hospital, where she underwent two surgeries. I conducted a computer search for any police reports generated between January 1, 2011, and February 20, 2012, containing blue pickup trucks with the listed partial license plates of 10N and 104N.

I did find three reports containing a blue truck with the partial license plate 10N. The first two were of no significance, but the third got my adrenaline pumping. This report was titled Sex Offender-Fail to Register report and was dated September 21, 2011. The suspect listed in that report was Andre Taylor, a black male born in 1974. Taylor was listed at 6'04, 195lbs, black hair, and brown eyes. Taylor was a level 3 Registered Sex Offender who was registered at an address in Puyallup, a city east of Tacoma. Taylor's vehicle was listed as a blue 1994 Dodge Dakota pickup truck, with a license plate of B96610N. In December 2011, a Felony Warrant for Fail to Register as a Sex Offender was issued for Taylor.

I contacted the Pierce County Sheriff's Detective, who wrote the Fail to Register report on Taylor. He confirmed that Taylor had not been seen by his wife since September and that Taylor's wife reported that Taylor took the listed truck when he left, and she did not know where he was living.

I looked up Taylor's history in the sex offender database and found the following listed in the public comments section:

"TAYLOR, Andre J. sex offender status stems from two convictions for rape in the third degree in Pierce County in 1996. According to official documents, Taylor showed up at the apartment of a known female and told her he needed a place to stay. She allowed him to stay. As she walked to her room to retire for the evening, Taylor followed her. She told Taylor to leave, but he pulled out a gun and held it to her head. The victim struggled with Taylor, and he hit her on the head three times with the gun. He then forced her to engage in sexual intercourse. Taylor continued to terrorize and stalk the victim after the rape. This incident resulted in Count I. Count II stems from an incident that occurred in 1995. Taylor went to the residence of a known 18-year-old female and woke her up. She invited Taylor inside and returned to bed. Taylor sat on the edge of the bed while they conversed. Taylor made advances toward the victim, and she told him to stop. Taylor pushed the victim down on the bed and threatened to shoot her if she didn't shut up. He proceeded to pull off her nightgown and sexually assaulted her. Taylor's other convictions include two burglaries and theft. One of the burglaries involved the victim in Count I. He returned to her home and was in the process of taking items when the police interrupted him. He has no other known sex offense history. Taylor denied raping his victims and was deemed non-amenable for treatment at the Sex Offender Treatment Program. He was placed in the Level III notification category and is considered a high risk to reoffend."

Based on Taylor's physical description, criminal history, and his vehicle description, including the license plate number, I issued a Wanted Person bulletin to area law enforcement agencies with a photo of Taylor and information about his Felony Warrant for Fail to Register as a Sex Offender.

That same afternoon, Detective Brian Vold and I contacted Susan Li at Tacoma General Hospital. A Tacoma Police Crime Scene Technician responded to photograph Susan's injuries, as well as collect saliva swabs and hair samples from Susan. After this was completed, Detective Vold and I conducted a recorded interview with Susan.

Susan told us she had just finished her shift as a crew trainer at a local fast-food restaurant. She left the building at 4:30 AM and began walking home alone in the dark. She noticed a blue truck driving back and forth on 72nd street. The driver slowed down and stared at her, but she ignored him and continued walking. The truck pulled into a parking lot and the driver watched her walk by his truck. After walking past, Susan crossed to the north side of 72nd and decided to take a shortcut through the Goodwill parking lot. She could see headlights coming up from behind her in the deserted lot and grabbed her cell phone. She got it unlocked, but before she could call 911, she looked behind her to see the truck coming right at her. She was struck on her right side and went completely underneath the truck. The suspect backed up, then got out and apologized for hitting her. Susan told us the man tried to pick her up from behind and told her he was going to take her to the hospital. She punched and screamed at him, causing him to back away. Susan tried to yell for help and flag a passing motorist, but no one stopped. Suddenly, a man walked up and asked if everything was alright. Susan couldn't move, but she asked the driver of the truck to pick up her cell phone that was in two pieces on the ground. Instead of calling for help, the suspect just stood there with Susan's phone. She snatched it from his hands and put the battery back in place so she could dial 911. As she was making the call, the suspect moved in front of his license plate to block her view. Susan said she was trying hard not to go unconscious and eventually handed the phone over to the passerby who'd walked up and intervened. At some point, the suspect got in his truck and drove away. Susan had never seen the suspect or the truck before that night.

She described the truck as a small blue 90's Chevy S-10 with the back window missing. She recalled the last three digits of the license plate were 10N.

Susan's injuries were significant and required multiple surgeries. She sustained several broken bones and had severe hemorrhages of both eyes, causing the whites of both of her eyes to turn solid red. She also had bruising all over her body.

On the afternoon of February 23, 2012, detectives received the phone records associated with the cell phone number being used by Andre Taylor. The subscriber for this phone number was a female who lived in the 3300 block of South Sawyer in the south end of Tacoma. Detectives drove to the Sawyer address and observed Taylor's truck, WA B96610N, backed into a parking stall next to the apartment. Surveillance was set up on the apartment. I contacted a prosecutor and briefed him on the case facts. He drafted a motion to amend the address on Taylor's Fail to Register warrant to the Sawyer address. I took the motion to a Judge, and she signed it. A short time later, Andre Taylor walked out of the Sawyer Street apartment and was detained by members of the Tacoma Police Gang Unit.

Taylor was transported to TPD Headquarters for an interview with Detective Larsen and his partner. During the interview, Taylor admitted he hit Susan with his truck, though he said it was an accident. He denied any intent to kidnap or sexually assault her.

Taylor was arrested and charged with Assault First Degree and Attempted Kidnapping Second Degree. At his trial, Andre Taylor was found guilty of Assault Second Degree with Sexual Motivation and Attempted Kidnapping Second Degree.

After receiving back-to-back CODIS hits linking Andre Taylor to two rapes that occurred a decade before, I got to work. I handled the follow-up investigation on Samantha Carmen, and Detective Brad Graham took the lead on Marci Bennet's case. After locating Samantha, I asked her to come to the station for an interview. She remembered the incident clearly, even though so many years had passed. Marci Bennet was a little more difficult to track down, but she too was located and agreed to participate in the prosecution.

Cold case investigations can be challenging. Memories fade, and evidence can be fleeting. I was shocked when our dispatch center was able to provide copies of the 911 calls from both incidents. Normally, 911 calls are only stored for a few months. One of the witnesses who'd been present with Samantha Carmen immediately after she was raped had a stroke in the years after the incident, and another told me to pound sand.

On September 5, 2014, Brad and I interviewed Andre Taylor at Coyote Ridge Correctional Facility in Connell, Washington. He denied any knowledge of either case and couldn't explain why his DNA would be found in both instances. When I showed him a photo of the white milky liquid left in the alley on Yakima Avenue, Taylor correctly identified it as semen. When I asked him who he thought it belonged to, he asked if it was his.

Even with all of the challenges, both cases were charged, and Andre Taylor was returned to Pierce County to await his trial. The two cases were tried together by Deputy Prosecuting Attorney Sven Nelson. Taylor opted for a bench trial; no jury, just the judge. He was found guilty of Rape First Degree, Rape Second Degree, and Robbery First Degree. On January 12, 2018, Andre Taylor was given an indeterminate sentence of 26 ½ years to life in prison. The Robbery conviction was later overturned based on the statute of limitations.

Now that Washington is working on testing every unsubmitted rape kit in the state, I have no doubt that more predators who thought they got away with it will be apprehended. My advice to those guys—sleep with one eye open.

CHAPTER 14

Jennifer Bastian

MAY 8, 2018.

It's an uncharacteristically sunny and warm afternoon in western Washington. I'm clicking away on my keyboard at my kitchen table when my phone rings. I look down at the caller ID to see the name Steve Reopelle, my replacement in the cold case unit. Steve had taken over for me upon my retirement a few weeks earlier.

"Hey, Steve, what's up?"

"Are you sitting down?"

The question sends a shiver down my spine. Questions that begin with, "are you sitting down?" usually lead to something bad.

I gulp in an unsuccessful attempt to quell the rising knot in my throat, then hesitantly reply, "Uh, yeah...why?"

"There's a match on Jennifer Bastian."

1986

Wulf Werner, a tall, stoic man with a thick German accent, was the lead detective on the Jennifer Bastian case, and he was determined to find her killer. A special task force was formed for the investigation. Based on the similarities between Jennifer's case and the unsolved murder of Michella Welch four months before Jennifer, it was believed that the same deranged predator was responsible for both killings. Thousands of tips were called in, leads were followed up, hundreds of suspects were interviewed. Hair, blood, and saliva samples were collected from persons of interest—all to no avail. Detectives zeroed in on one particular man who behaved oddly, drove a van, and frequented the park. This individual was eventually ruled out by DNA.

The investigation continued for several years, but eventually, the leads dried up. Detective Werner continued to follow up on tips over the years until he retired in 2008. I saw him from time to time after he left, and he always made a point to ask me about Jennifer's case. Even though he'd retired, the case was a part of him, and he couldn't let it go. I would eventually come to know that feeling all too well.

COLD CASE INVESTIGATION

2009 was an exciting year. The highlight was the birth of my daughter. I took about five months off for maternity leave.

My first day back in the saddle was a real shit show. I barely stepped foot in my cubicle when Detective Gene Miller walked up and said, "Hey, you don't have anything going, right?" Rhetorical question. "Can you go out and do a canvas?"

Gene and I had partnered together on many cases over the years. I was initially stunned by his lack of sensitivity. In my head, I thought, "What the fuck?" I'd just walked in the door after being gone for five months. Maybe start with "Hi, how are you?" But then I snapped back into reality and remembered…that's Gene.

Turns out there had been an officer-involved shooting by a Pierce County Sheriff's Deputy within the city limits. That meant the TPD Homicide Unit was tasked with investigating.

I should have taken a few more days off.

I spent a couple of hours knocking on doors and talking to the neighbors. I don't remember if I actually gleaned any useful information or if it was the usual "I don't know shit, I didn't see shit, and I didn't do shit" routine—probably the latter. I was still nursing, so by the time I made it back to the station, I had leaked through my shirt and had two soggy milk stains spreading across my chest. I gagged at the thought of pumping in the locker room or bathroom. I'm kind of a germaphobe. The saving grace was that while Gene could be gruff and seemingly insensitive at times, he let me turn his office into my pumping station. I set up a small refrigerator and was able to pump in privacy. I loved him for that.

The other exciting event in 2009 was the creation of the Tacoma Police Department Cold Case Unit. Gene headed up the unit, which began with more than two hundred and fifty unsolved homicide cases on the books in Tacoma. The Jennifer Bastian and Michella Welch cases were the primary inspiration for creating the new unit. As a young patrol officer, Gene had been assigned to work on the cases while recovering from ankle surgery on light duty. The cases left a lasting impression on the young officer, and he was driven to solve them when he became the cold case detective decades later.

When I returned from maternity leave, I began working on cold cases as collateral duty and spent many hours reviewing Jennifer's case with Gene.

Just like I had done as a new detective, I studied the macabre crime scene photos. They were still the worst I'd ever seen—and I've seen some pretty horrific shit. The terror she must have felt during her last moments on earth was something I couldn't shake. Those images, coupled with my terrifying childhood recollection of the crime, motivated me to work that much harder to find out who killed her.

I had the opportunity to meet Ralph and Pattie Bastian for the first time in 2013. I could tell they still desperately wanted answers. Gene and I had stopped by the Bastian home one afternoon to collect a few photos of Jennifer for an upcoming case review. As we were leaving, Ralph grabbed onto Gene's arm and said he didn't have much more time and implored us to find out who'd killed Jennifer. That moment was absolutely gut-wrenching.

Gene and I took a trip to the National Center for Missing and Exploited Children (NCMEC) in Alexandria, Virginia, in May of 2013 to present the case to a panel of experts. The case review was orchestrated by retired FBI Profiler Jennifer Eakin, who took a position as a case manager at NCMEC after retiring from the Bureau. Jen and I had kept in contact over the years since the Zina Linnik case, and she thought the Jennifer Bastian investigation would be a good candidate for a case review.

The panel consisted of about twenty subject matter experts, including renowned FBI Profiler Kenneth Lanning, a guru in the area of crimes against children. Current and former FBI agents with expertise in crimes against children, detectives from Washington DC, NCMEC case managers, and consultants, many of whom were retired law enforcement specializing in crimes against children, also attended the review. Additionally, two Forensic Scientists sat on the panel. A former Section Chief of the Scientific Analysis Section of the FBI Crime Lab and Dr. Angela Williamson was the Unknown Victim Identification Program Manager at NCMEC. Prior to that, Angela was the Director of Forensic Casework at Bode Technologies, a private DNA lab. Angela and I shared a passion for using DNA to solve cold cases, and over the next several years, we became good friends, corresponding about stray serial killers and all things DNA. The case review was extremely beneficial and gave us some new investigative ideas.

After we returned from the NCMEC case review, Gene submitted Jennifer's swimsuit to the crime lab for DNA testing in the hopes of developing a reference sample of Jennifer's DNA. He also sent hairs found at the crime scene to the Minnesota

Department of Public Safety Crime Lab for mitochondrial DNA testing. Mitochondrial DNA is passed down from a mother to her children, but only the female children pass it on to their children. This type of DNA testing was used in cases where nuclear DNA is not possible.

In the case of the foreign hairs found on the ground with Jennifer's body, they didn't have any root material adhering to them for nuclear DNA testing, so mitochondrial testing was the next best option at that time.

There's no criminal database to upload and search mitochondrial DNA, so you need to have a sample from a suspect for comparison. The Minnesota lab obtained mitochondrial DNA from the hairs and concluded they were concordant, meaning they could not be excluded as having originated from a common source. They were excluded as belonging to Jennifer. At that point, we had no mitochondrial DNA from any suspects for comparison, but it was a good piece of information to have for the future.

In November 2013, Gene got a call from a Forensic Scientist at the crime lab. He asked Gene if he was interested in the male DNA found in Jennifer's swimsuit. This was an attempt at humor, I think. The scientist went on to tell Gene that a single source male DNA profile was generated from semen located in the crotch of Jennifer's swimsuit, which was found around her ankle.

This was a shock.

It appeared that the original investigators made an assumption that Jennifer was likely sexually assaulted after her bathing suit was removed; therefore, it would be unlikely to find the suspect's DNA on her swimsuit. The new test results told a different story.

The DNA profile was entered into CODIS, but there was no match in the state or national database. To everyone's surprise, the DNA profile did not match the suspect DNA profile from the murder of Michella Welch either. These shocking new DNA results told us we were looking for two separate killers, and it appeared that the two cases were unrelated.

The new DNA results changed everything.

First off, there were dozens of suspects who had previously been eliminated because they were in jail or prison during one of the murders. Therefore it was assumed they could be excluded from both under the premise that one man was responsible for both crimes. You have to remember that this crime occurred in 1986 when all police reports were typed on a typewriter or handwritten. None of the reports from the massive case file were digitized.

Gene began compiling a list of suspects that had not been eliminated with DNA. Detectives collected voluntary DNA samples from a couple of dozen suspects and sent them to the crime lab for DNA testing. One by one, they were all eliminated.

We asked the crime lab to send the unknown suspect DNA profile to the CODIS Manager in every other state with a request to do a keyboard search of the profile in the individual state databases. We did this because we knew that not all DNA profiles entered into a state DNA database are eligible for the national database. We hoped we might get a match to a case from another state that hadn't made it to the national database. Unfortunately, we got no matches.

I spent months searching our old records database, CLEAR, looking for any possible linkage to Jennifer's case. I requested dozens of old reports that I dug out of the system by entering the old codes used to classify reports in the system that had been in use from 1979 to 1999. The system contained some basic information from police reports that had been written during the time the system was in use.

I searched classification codes like "kidnap" or "sex crime" and added, "wooded" or "outdoor" to the premise field. I was able to filter the search by census block and district if I wanted to search a particular location in the city of Tacoma. I was also able to search for cases in unincorporated Pierce County. I would read the location, names, and ages of suspects and victims, and sometimes I could see if a weapon was used. I would write down the case number and then email a list of cases to the South Sound 911 records manager asking for copies of the reports from archives. I would read the reports, and if there was a named suspect or arrestee, I would run a background check on them to see what else they'd been up to. I would check the suspect's criminal history, and if he had no DNA in CODIS, I might add him to the list for DNA collection, depending on what he'd done.

The scariest part of this process was that each criminal history was worse than the previous I'd read. Just when I thought, "Dang, this has to be the guy!" Someone else would appear on my screen with an even more frightening past.

As an example of how consumed I became with Jennifer's case, I would take notes while watching true crime TV shows like *Forensic Files* or *Dateline*. If I learned about a suspect who'd committed a crime similar to the 1986 Tacoma slaying during one of these programs, I would write down the information and then run a criminal history check on the suspect when I got back to work.

I knew that serial offenders are highly mobile and thought the suspect might have committed crimes in other states as well. If I couldn't confirm that DNA was in CODIS for one of these guys, I might add the name to my growing list of potential suspects.

In January 2015, Detective Gene Miller retired, and I took over as the cold case detective. Over the next few years, Pattie, Jennifer's mother, and I got to know each other better, and she would eventually volunteer her time to help me in the Cold Case Unit. Tragically, Jennifer's dad, Ralph, passed away in 2015 without finding out who'd killed his baby girl.

That year, I heard about an innovative technique that identified a surname from Y-chromosome DNA, ultimately leading to the identification of a suspect in two cold case homicides from the early 1990s in Phoenix. I got the name of the woman who'd assisted Phoenix PD with the case and decided to give it a try. Her name was Dr. Colleen Fitzpatrick; a rocket scientist turned genealogist and founder of Identifinders International. I reached out to Fitzpatrick and discussed my case with her. After learning about the process, I asked the Washington State Patrol Crime Lab to obtain a Y-STR DNA profile from the DNA evidence in Jennifer's case.

I sent the Y-STR profile to Dr. Fitzpatrick so that she could conduct her analysis, looking for a last name associated with the paternal line related to the Y-STR profile. This information could be used as an investigative lead in an attempt to identify the unknown offender. Dr. Fitzpatrick searched thousands of public Y-STR genealogy databases looking for matches to the DNA profile in my case and provided me with a report containing three last names or surnames associated with the Y-STR profile from the Jennifer Bastian case, including Washburn, Smith, and Holbrook.

Y-chromosome DNA is passed down from father to son along the paternal line, so men sharing the same Y-STR profile should also share the same last name. Exceptions include adoptions where the male child takes the adopted father's last name or boys who take their mother's surname. Children conceived as a result of a secret affair would be included here too.

While I found the information interesting, I wasn't convinced that it was useful. This was a new technique for law enforcement, and I had only heard of two other police agencies who'd tried this technique. Phoenix PD had been successful in closing in on a suspect thanks to the information provided by Dr. Fitzpatrick, but the other had not. I searched the case file for the last names given by Dr. Fitzpatrick and found there were no men with the name Holbrook, and given the commonality of the last name Smith, I wasn't optimistic about that one.

I found only one man with the surname Washburn in the case file—Robert Washburn.

In May 1986, Robert Washburn had called in a tip about a suspect in Michella Welch's murder which had occurred several months before Jennifer's death. In the tip, he reported seeing a man in Point Defiance Park who matched the description of a composite sketch. The tip was called in three months *before* Jennifer was murdered. Washburn was interviewed by detectives in December 1986. They found nothing suspicious about him and moved on to other leads.

Aside from searching the case file, I also checked the local records database for the last names provided by Dr. Fitzpatrick but found no one who piqued my interest. I also worked with Dr. Barbara Rae-Venter a couple of years later but wasn't able to make any further progress with the case, due to the level of DNA degradation.

In August of 2015, I began working with Parabon Nanolabs in Virginia. This company offered a cutting-edge type of DNA testing called phenotyping, which can identify characteristics based on DNA, such as ancestry, hair, skin and eye color, facial morphology, and freckling. Parabon then used a forensic artist to create a composite of what the suspect may have looked like based on the DNA results.

The first round of testing at Parabon was not successful in Jennifer's case due to DNA degradation. A second round was attempted and was successful. I received the results in September 2015.

The suspect was determined to be 51.03% Central Eastern European and 43.43% Northwest European with blue or green eyes and blonde or red hair, fair or very fair-skinned, and few/some freckling. A computer-generated composite image of what the suspect may have looked like at age twenty-five was created as well.

By the beginning of 2016, there was still no DNA match to any of the suspects who provided voluntary DNA samples. I submitted Jennifer's white Aerobix tennis shoes to our Forensics Lab with a request to attempt to identify latent fingerprints from their exterior surface. Unfortunately, none were found. I decided that the case file was unmanageable in its current state, so I undertook the daunting task of hand entering every male who appeared in the massive case file into a web-based, searchable database. The system, called Web EOC, was originally designed to help the Pierce County Department of Emergency Management handle emergencies and disasters. A new version of the system was created as a lead management system for our Child Abduction Response Team (CART) by Pierce County IT personnel, and they agreed to modify it for me so that I could use it for the Bastian cold case.

I painstakingly read every report, note, teletype, patient list, offender list, Field Information Report, and a scrap of paper contained within the Bastian case file. I created a record for each male found within the case file. Each entry included the name and any identifying info I could find. I also included the date of the report in which they appeared and who wrote the report. I included a short narrative about why they were in the file, and I added criminal history, photos, and any other pertinent info. I included whether they had DNA in CODIS or if we had collected their DNA as a part of the investigation.

I was able to prioritize suspects from high to low, and I was able to filter based on several criteria. I was also able to eliminate people in the database. I only eliminated a person by DNA or confirmed incarceration at the time of the murder. This process took about three months to complete. When I finished, there were more than twenty-three-hundred names in the database, and only about three-hundred and fifty had been eliminated by DNA or incarceration.

I didn't have a partner assigned to work with me in the Cold Case Unit, but I did have quite a bit of help from the FBI. Aside from funding all of the DNA work that had been completed by Identifinders and Parabon, FBI Special Agent Terry Postma opened an FBI case and agreed to work with me on the investigation. We spent months creating background packets for each suspect we wanted to locate and collect DNA from. Terry also tracked down and collected DNA samples from several elusive suspects on our list, including two brothers he tracked down in Oregon.

2016 was the thirty-year anniversary of the murder of Jennifer Bastian. I was also required to organize an annual exercise for our Child Abduction Response Team (CART). I decided on a kind of hybrid cold case CART exercise consisting of a two-day CART activation for our team that would focus on the case. Instead of an AMBER Alert, we held a press conference on the morning of the first day. At the press conference, our Public Information Officer unveiled a poster containing the digital composite image of the unknown suspect created by Parabon. We staffed a tip line and assigned more than sixty people to the two-day operation. Half of the detectives and FBI Agents were assigned to follow up on new tips that were called in, while the other half were assigned by Special Agent Terry Postma to collect voluntary DNA samples from high-priority suspects who appeared in the case file.

Overall, the operation was a success. More than one hundred and twenty new tips were called into the tip line during the exercise. We received local and national media attention and collected forty new voluntary DNA samples from potential suspects.

After the exercise, we continued to collect DNA samples from men listed in the case file, thanks to overtime funding provided by the US Marshals Service. I tracked down blood spot cards from the autopsy for several deceased suspects for DNA testing as well. Special Agent Postma sent out leads to FBI field offices around the country requesting DNA collections from several dozen out-of-state persons of interest in the case file.

After several months of pounding the pavement, TPD detectives had collected 121 new DNA samples, and FBI agents collected an additional forty samples from out-of-state persons of interest.

The DNA collection process was memorable, to say the least.

Many of the potential suspects in the case file were living off the grid, so to speak. Some were homeless, and one was a carnie working for a traveling circus. One guy was living in a trailer in Lakewood that could have been mistaken for the city dump. As Detective Brad Graham and I pulled down the gravel driveway to contact him, we were greeted with a stockpile of trash, junk, furniture, and other miscellaneous implements, which formed a veritable mountain of shit next to the trailer. We stepped around the trash installation to reach the front door.

Initially, I'd planned to speak to the man inside; but once he opened the door, there was a change of plans. First, there was the smell.

Now granted, I'd been doing this job for a long time and had encountered my share of filth. I kept a bottle of Febreze in my trunk, so I could decontaminate before getting back into my car after leaving the latest hovel reeking of any combination of cigarette smoke, body odor, crack, and usually marijuana. But, If I didn't have to go inside, I wouldn't.

In this case, the odor was strike one.

Strike two—the gallon jug of yellow liquid (assuming it was pee) on the "coffee table."

We decided to talk outside.

After explaining why we were there, he signed my consent

form and let me swab his mouth.

Another candidate was the last known to be living in Hoquiam, so Special Agent Postma and I drove down to the Washington Coast in search of the man. We knocked on the door at the address on his license but found he didn't live there. Next, we drove over to the neighboring city of Aberdeen—the hometown of the late Nirvana frontman, Kurt Cobain. We stopped in at the Police Department to ask if there were any recent contacts with the man we were looking for. The secretary knew his name as soon as we said it and told us an officer could lead us to where he was staying. We followed the officer to a desolate stretch of road where the man was living in his van, down by the river (no shit).

The inside of the van was so completely crammed full of crap that the driver's seat appeared to be the only space available for him to sit. He was quite a character. Even though he only had a few teeth, he managed to pay me a compliment by saying, "They didn't have FBI Agents that looked like you when I was younger." He provided a DNA sample without any trouble. I didn't have the heart to tell him I wasn't an FBI Agent.

In August 2016, I attended the International Homicide Investigators Association symposium in New Orleans. Dr. Angela Williamson and I gave a presentation on missing offender DNA samples in CODIS, my passion project. At that time, I had a strong belief that the key to solving not just Jennifer's case, but potentially many more, was the collection of DNA samples from convicted offenders who'd slipped through the cracks.

In 2017, I submitted the ligature found around Jennifer's neck to the Washington State Patrol Crime Lab in an attempt to identify the type of rope and any information that could be gleaned. The lab determined the rope to be a 67" by 1/8" diameter piece of cotton twine.

During this same time period, I began sending the DNA

samples collected during the CART activation and the months following to the lab for DNA testing. I sent just over one hundred of the DNA reference samples to a private lab and the remainder to the WSP Crime Lab for testing.

After waiting for months, the first batch from the private lab came back all negative (no matches). The second batch went to the state crime lab. After several more months, I got a report from the lab stating none of the samples were a match. The third batch had the same result. No matches.

I sent the final batch of eighteen samples to the WSP Crime Lab on January 4, 2018, with little hope for a match. I was pretty discouraged by that point. There were so many promising suspects that looked good—right up to the point they were eliminated with DNA.

This is where my involvement as a Tacoma Police Detective ends. In April 2018, I decided to take a job with the Washington State Attorney General's Office as an investigator for the Sexual Assault Kit Initiative. In 2017, the AGO won a $3 million federal grant to inventory and test unsubmitted sexual assault kits across the state of Washington.

At the time, I was burned out. I had been on-call for the previous fourteen years, and I was sick of the call-outs and tired of working without a partner. Though I had a couple of cold case homicides charged in 2018, I was frustrated with my job. Working on cold cases can be like swimming against the current. There's a whole lot of spinning your wheels, and results can be elusive. I was especially apprehensive about telling Pattie Bastian about my departure.

Pattie and I had become close over the years, and she was a great inspiration and motivator for me. I'm continuously amazed by her strength and ability to remain positive despite her personal tragedy. Making the decision to leave TPD after twenty-one years was difficult. Leaving without solving Jennifer's case was painful.

My last day of work as a Tacoma Police Officer was April 13, 2018. Reality began to set in after I turned in my assigned car and my gear. My unit took me out to lunch, and then my supervisor drove me home. My sergeant was a second-generation TPD Officer I'd known most of my life. His father retired as an Assistant Chief and I spent many days, nights, and weekends at his house since his younger sister, Kristin, and I were close friends in school. I managed to keep from bursting into tears until after he left my house.

I started my new job with the Attorney General's Office on April 16. The new job was going great, and I really liked the people I was working with. I enjoy creating things from the ground up, and even though I felt like I was drinking from a fire hose, this project was a worthwhile challenge.

On the afternoon of May 8, 2018, I was working from home when my phone buzzed. The caller was Detective Steve Reopelle, my replacement in the cold case unit. When I answered the phone, he asked me if I was sitting down.

"Uh, yeah...why?"

"There's a match on Jennifer Bastian," he said.

I don't exactly remember what was said next. I do remember the emotion bubbling up in my throat and not being able to get any words out. Then there were the silent tears. When I finally felt like I could squeak out a few words, I asked for the guy's name.

"Robert Washburn."

Robert Washburn was listed in the original case file because he called in a tip nearly three months before Jennifer was killed. On May 14, 1986, he phoned in a tip saying he recognized a sketch of the suspect as someone he had seen near the rhododendron garden at Point Defiance Park. Detectives attempted to contact Washburn several times without success. Detective Wulf Werner was able to interview Washburn at his home in the 3100 block of North Huson Street on December 15, 1986. During that interview, Washburn said he'd jogged the trails off the Five Mile Drive at Point Defiance Park, probably twice a day. He said he jogged the trails prior to Jennifer being discovered and recalled smelling the odor but didn't know what it was. He also said he was in the park the day it was cordoned off.

Washburn gave a detailed description of the man he said resembled the sketch from the Welch case. He said he'd seen the man in Point Defiance Park several times and would get his license plate and call it in the next time he saw him.

Washburn only had one previous arrest for criminal trespass and vehicle prowling in King County from December 1985 and really wasn't a good suspect…on paper. When interviewed by detectives in 1986, he reported being laid off from his job at a local laboratory at the time of the murder. He was listed in the report as an "Other," not a "Suspect," and the report was classified as low-priority while the investigators moved on to evaluate more promising leads.

The only reason I added Robert Washburn to the DNA collection list was because of his last name—Washburn. It was one of the surnames given to me by Dr. Fitzpatrick based on her search of the Y chromosome DNA databases. After receiving the request from Special Agent Terry Postma, FBI Agents knocked on Washburn's door and collected a voluntary DNA sample from him at his apartment in Illinois on March 6, 2017. Washburn was a white male with green eyes, which is consistent with the phenotyping predictions made by Parabon Nanolabs. That's it. His criminal history didn't stand out. There were hundreds of others in the case file who looked much more promising, based on their documented history as a sexual deviant.

Washburn's name would never have been in the case file had he not inserted himself into the investigation by calling in that tip.

The bizarre part is that he inserted himself several months *before* he committed the murder.

According to the Washington State Child Abduction Murder study, 10 % of the suspects interjected themselves into the investigation somehow, and 9.7 % of suspects contacted the police or media. 23.7 % of the suspects returned to the body disposal site. I suspect Robert Washburn did too.

The realization that Robert Washburn's DNA was a match to the semen found in the crotch of Jennifer Bastian's swimsuit was surreal. It was also a good lesson for me. First, when it comes to cold case homicides, the suspect's name is usually in the case file. Second, he may be listed in the file as someone benign, like a neighbor or witness, not necessarily a suspect.

It's difficult to describe how much this case meant to so many people, including me. Most people probably thought it would never be solved. I hoped that perhaps clearing the untested rape kit backlog might provide a match someday, or maybe there would be a cold hit in CODIS.

I never imagined there would be a DNA match twenty-five days after I retired.

After talking to Detective Reopelle on the phone, I stood in my living room and stared out the window across the blue water of the Narrows to the tree-lined cliffs of Point Defiance Park.

"Jennifer, you were not forgotten," I said to myself.

My husband, Ed, was home sick that day.

I was shaking as I woke him up to tell him the amazing news. I threw on a sweater and two matching shoes (I think) and scrambled down to the station to help Detective Reopelle sort through the massive case file looking for the reports pertinent to Washburn. As I climbed the familiar staircase to the second floor, I saw my old boss standing on the landing above me with tears in his eyes. He gave me a hug, and I tried hard to keep from crying myself.

The most difficult part of the days that followed was keeping the news from Pattie Bastian. I'd already invited her to have Mother's Day brunch with my family that coming Sunday, and I dreaded the idea of sitting across the table from her with this life-altering secret. The plan was for TPD detectives to fly to Illinois the following day to get eyes on Washburn. Pattie would be notified as soon as he was in custody. We wanted to make the notification to Pattie in person, but I wasn't sure when that would be or if she was even in town. I dialed her number, ostensibly to say, "Hi." and catch up. Thankfully, she had no plans to be away that week. That was good.

As for me, well, let's just say that my stomach was in knots, I couldn't sleep, and I was on an emotional rollercoaster. The only people I could talk to about what was happening were Ed and Detective Steve Reopelle. One minute I was crying, and in the next moment, I was overcome with self-doubt. I doubted my decision to leave TPD at that point and regretted not being able to arrest Jennifer's killer myself.

Robert Washburn was arrested for Murder First Degree at his apartment in Eureka, Illinois, on the morning of Thursday, May 10. I was at TPD headquarters when the arrest was made.

Once Washburn was in custody, Assistant Chief Shawn Gustason and I drove to Pattie Bastian's home to give her the news (Police Chief Don Ramsdell was out of town). It was about 8 AM when we arrived at her doorstep. Her little dog, Zoe, came out yapping like crazy when we knocked. Pattie answered the door and looked a little confused. We had clearly woken her up, and she had no idea why I was at her house at that hour. She also had never met the tall man in uniform standing next to me.

I'd tried to rehearse what I planned to say to Pattie that morning, but I couldn't remember any of it. All I could choke out was, "We got him." At that point, Pattie looked a little unsteady. I reached out to her and hugged her for a long moment while we both shed a few tears.

After asking a couple of questions, Pattie called her daughter, Theresa, in Texas so that I could give her the news. I spent the rest of the day with Pattie, a luxury I wouldn't have had if I had still been working the case. We called the original lead detective on Jennifer's case, Wulf Werner, and gave him the news—he was overwhelmed with happiness.

Without a doubt, it was the best day of my career.

I remember calling my mom and breaking the news to her. I think she cried more than I did. The other thing that I remember are the calls and messages that I got from friends, telling me how Jennifer's death had affected them so deeply as children and how happy they were to hear the case had been solved.

Jennifer's sister, Theresa, flew in from Texas for a press conference at Tacoma Police Headquarters on May 14. Her visit meant she was able to join us for a truly memorable Mother's Day brunch.

Washburn declined to be interviewed by Detectives Steve Reopelle and Ryan Larsen after his arrest in Illinois. After being told that his DNA linked him to the murder, he said, "I did not kill that little girl." He also made the following interesting statement, "Just want to make sure my daughter's safe and I'd like to know how I went from suspect…I mean, my DNA was all over that park."

Shortly after the arrest, an inmate in the jail contacted police and said he had spoken to Washburn while they were in jail together, and Washburn had admitted to raping and killing Jennifer Bastian. The inmate reported that Washburn backpedaled after the admission and said he came across her bike and hid it in the bushes; then, he looked around and found Jennifer's body nearby and masturbated over her body. According to the inmate, Washburn later changed his story back and admitted he raped and strangled Jennifer. The inmate said Washburn told him he was jogging in the park and had been looking for sex. The inmate said Washburn described himself as a "Sick, kinky fuck." The inmate said Washburn described Jennifer as "exquisite" and "beautiful" and said he couldn't help himself. He said Washburn indicated he had been keeping track of Jennifer's family and knew her father had passed away the previous year. The inmate said Washburn told him he wanted the death penalty and that he didn't want his family to know what he had done.

For close to nine months, Robert Washburn sat in the Pierce County Jail awaiting his trial. At some point, he decided he wanted to plead guilty, which was a welcome relief to Pattie and Theresa.

On January 25, 2018, I saw Robert Washburn for the first time in person after he pled guilty to Murder First Degree. He was seated in court next to his attorney while Pattie and Theresa Bastian were telling the judge how the loss of Jennifer had affected their lives over the previous thirty-two years. I don't think there was a dry eye in the courtroom that afternoon. From the judge to one of the cameramen filming the hearing, everyone was affected by the family's powerfully emotional words.

I was standing beside Pattie and Theresa and had my first opportunity to look directly at Robert Washburn. I was confused because he didn't look at all like the depraved rapist and killer I had imagined in my mind over the past three decades. He looked unremarkable and pathetic. He kept his head down and never looked up once during their moving testimony.

After they spoke, we returned to the gallery, and the judge sentenced him to the maximum allowed by law in 1986—26.6 years in prison. As he was led out of the courtroom, he received a fitting farewell from Theresa Bastian in the words of Ice Cube: "Bye, Felicia."

For years, I couldn't drive around the North end of Tacoma without picking out men and thinking, "Could that be him?" I would see a man in a store or coffee shop and wonder if he could be the killer. If I saw a guy who looked a little off in a park, my antennae went up. This became so automatic that I was still doing it after the arrest was made. The thought would pop into my head, and then I would have to remind myself that it was over.

After three long decades, the citizens of Tacoma and the families and friends of Jennifer Bastian finally got the justice they deserved. Was it closure? I don't think so. From what I'm told, there is no such thing—Jennifer is still gone. For me personally, I feel honored to have been able to contribute to the resolution of a case that had such an impact on an entire community—and on me as a little girl.

In 2019, Jennifer and Michella's Law was passed into law in Washington. It took me several years of working with state legislators, testifying in front of various legislative committees, and garnering community support along with media attention to finally get House Bill 1326 passed into law. Washington State Representatives Brad Klippert and Tina Orwall, along with Pattie and Theresa Bastian, and Pattie's niece, April, played pivotal roles in getting this important law passed.

Jennifer and Michella's Law strengthens Washington's DNA collection law by adding additional qualifying offenses which require submission of a DNA sample upon conviction. The law also allows law enforcement to submit DNA from deceased convicted felons to CODIS, regardless of conviction date. This piece is so important for cold case investigations because many of the suspects responsible for cold cases may be deceased and likely never had their DNA collected prior to death—either because they were convicted before the DNA law took effect or they died before it became retroactive for those in prison. I believe Jennifer and Michella's Law will make a significant impact on cold case investigations in the future.

*Note: The details of Michella Welch's murder investigation were not included in this book because the suspect was awaiting trial at the time of this writing.

CHAPTER 15

In My DNA

M y hair. Where to begin…

Throughout my life, my hair has been a source of confusion, mystery, and wonder to many—including myself. Once, when I was getting my hair cut, the Korean shop owner walked over and began inspecting my hair. She looked at it up close, then touched it, but seemed genuinely perplexed. Finally, she barked, "You got white people hair…what are you?"

That's the thing about my hair. To the untrained observer, it may look like typical Caucasian hair when it's been tamed with a flat iron. However, it would be a huge mistake to treat my mane as such. My hair is naturally curly, and the texture is fine.

Time after time, I'd go for a haircut with a new stylist and ask them flat out if they knew how to deal with ethnic hair. Sometimes they said yes, when in fact, they had no idea what they were dealing with.

Shortly after Jennifer Bastian's killer pled guilty, I agreed to participate in a couple of television shows highlighting the investigation. During one of the shows, the hair and makeup lady was trying to make me HD-camera ready. I had already spent a significant amount of time at home making sure my hair looked good—way more time than I normally spent on my hair—with soft beachy waves I was actually happy with. To my horror, the woman pulled out something that looked like a dog brush and began combing my hair out. I wanted to jump out of my skin and scream. I asked her what she was doing, but she assured me that my hair was going to look great—it just needed to be smoothed out for the camera. Well shit. Had I known this, I would have flat ironed my hair and avoided the whole disaster. Instead, my soft curls had been brushed into odd 70's style waves. I thought it looked like hammered dog shit.

I was taking no chances with the second show, which was filmed in New York, and decided to make an appointment at Dry Bar for a blowout before filming. The stylist was black (thank you, Jesus), and she did a fabulous job on my hair.

My sister, Casey, was with me in NYC and told my stylist why we were there. The young woman was impressed and told me that I didn't look like a detective (I get that a lot). She asked me all kinds of questions about Tacoma—what was the crime rate like, what kinds of murders were common there. I told her most murders in Tacoma were drug or gang-related. She responded, "Dang....so you in the hood." I laughed and said it really wasn't that bad.

As she washed my hair, we continued to chat about the show and our plans for the day. Out of nowhere, I was jolted up almost out of my seat as she turned ice-cold water onto my scalp. I wasn't prepared for that and squealed, "Whoa…that's freezing!"

She laughed and said, "Girl, you be lookin' at dead bodies—you can handle some cold water on your head."

As the cold water was pouring onto my scalp, I laughed, and at that moment, I realized she was right. I was a strong woman who'd been faced with countless obstacles over the years and always kept moving forward. I thought back to my shaky start in life—a three-pound preemie born to a single teenage mother. I guess you could say I was a fighter from the beginning.

Being a detective who also happened to be a female of color gave me a unique perspective on the crimes I investigated and the interactions I had with victims and their families. I recall the family of one of my homicide victims initially making the assumption that nothing would be done to solve the murder because the victim was "just another black man." That couldn't have been further from the truth, and after several years, I proved the family wrong and solved the case.

Being a female detective also illuminated the double standard set for women in my business. A few years ago, I testified in front of my state legislature about the need for improved DNA laws. My captain accompanied me to the hearing and introduced himself at the beginning of my testimony. When I was done speaking, one of the legislators thanked me for my presentation, then thanked my captain for coming to "hold my hand."

While sitting in that salon chair, my mind flashed through all the experiences that impacted my life and made me the *detective* I came to be. I thought about the stranger at the end of my bed and, a few years later, learned about the rape and murder of Jennifer Bastian, followed by my fascination with the atrocities committed by Ted Bundy. These life experiences sparked my desire to seek justice, specifically for those most vulnerable in society. And while I dealt with some instances of sexism and racism along the way, I always soldiered on and kept my eye on my goals—seeking justice for victims and their families.

I have since retired from police work, and while I do sleep a little easier at night (no more 2 AM call-outs for gang shootings and drug-related murders), my desire to seek justice will never leave me.

I no longer carry a gun and badge, but admittedly, I still possess that deeply ingrained paranoia. I don't let my kid walk to the neighbor's house or ride her bike without a GPS tracker for fear of her being kidnapped, and I rarely make it through a true crime show without Googling the killer to see what other cases he might be responsible for. I may never respond to another crime scene, but seeking justice will always be in my DNA.

About the Author

Lindsey Wade is a retired detective with an impressive track record of utilizing her keen investigative instincts and DNA to solve violent crimes. After retiring from the Tacoma Police Department, Lindsey joined the Washington State Attorney General's Office as a Senior Investigator assigned to the Sexual Assault Kit Initiative to pursue her passion—using DNA to solve cold cases. In 2019, Lindsey worked with state legislators to pass a new DNA law in Washington known as Jennifer & Michella's Law. As a subject matter expert, Lindsey has been a speaker at numerous law enforcement conferences around the country, lecturing on cold cases, sex crimes, DNA, and child abduction response.

Acknowledgments

I want to take this opportunity to thank the unsung heroes of this book - The Washington State Patrol Crime Laboratory Forensic Scientists who diligently worked behind the scenes to uncover the truth in these cases. First, Forensic Scientist Jeremy Sanderson, who worked on many of my cases over the years, including Jennifer Bastian's, testing countless pieces of evidence and hundreds of DNA reference samples from potential suspects.

I also want to recognize retired DNA Supervisor Chris Sewell who worked on many of my cases. I know Chris truly cared about his work and he always made time to discuss a case or entertain one of my crazy ideas.

I also want to thank retired CODIS Manager Jean Johnston. You provided me with a wealth of knowledge related to DNA and CODIS. I suspect you cringed when you saw my number pop up on your caller ID, but you always took the time to discuss my DNA questions. You also spent a significant amount of time helping me eliminate suspects from the Jennifer Bastian and Michella Welch cases by checking to see if a person on my list had DNA in CODIS here in Washington or in some other state. I am truly grateful to you, Jean.

Forensic Scientists rarely get credit for the exacting, tedious, time-consuming work they do. Without these dedicated professionals, most of the crimes in this book would never have been solved. None of the victims would have justice and none of their families would have answers. To my former partners from my Patrol days: Shaun Moore, Rob Hannity, and Ron Bieker: Thanks for the crazy memories on patrol and for always having my back.

Von Narcisse: Thinking back to our stranger-than-fiction times in Patrol always makes me smile and sometimes shudder. I have so much admiration and respect for you, and I really wish you were still in T-Town.

Barb Justice: Thank you for introducing me to the wild world of police work and starting me on my law enforcement journey.

Pattie Bastian: Your strength and poise are an inspiration to many, most of all me. I am so lucky to have you in my life.

Theresa Bastian: I have loved our conversations over the years, and I am truly grateful to call you my friend.

Lindsey Smith: You took a chance on me and I'm so glad you did. I not only gained an amazing agent and publisher, but I also gained a true friend.

Dawn Ius: This book would not have become what it is without your guidance and encouragement. Thank you.

Mary Robnett: You have been such an important role model and mentor to me, thank you.

Sgt. Tom Davidson and Assistant Chief Rich McCrea: Thank you for making me the lead detective on one of the most challenging cases of my career—even though it felt like a trial by fire. It was my first homicide as the lead detective, but your strong faith in my investigative abilities allowed me to grow as a detective and prove my worthiness as a homicide investigator.

Amy Scanlon, Phoebe Mulligan, Louise Nist, Stefanie Avery, and Gretchen Aguirre: I never would have made it through my career in one piece without our walks to Starbucks, wine-infused debriefs, and your amazing friendships.

Brad and Gene: You two are my ride-or-die. Gene, working

with you made all the bad shit a little easier to stomach. Brad, we were partners for years, but you'll be my brother for life.

Neil Kirkpatrick: Thank you for listening.

I'm grateful to the Tacoma Police Department for making my dream of becoming a police officer a reality back when I was just a twenty-one-year-old kid. I had an amazing career with TPD. The experiences were unparalleled. The lifelong friendships I made are priceless.

Mom: You are my loudest cheerleader, my number one fan, and my very first friend. I love you.

Dad: Thank you for teaching me to be confident in myself and for your unwavering love and support. I love you.

Tony and Casey: I'm lucky to have the best siblings ever, and to be able to call you my friends. You are both amazing people and love you more than you could imagine.

Ed: You are my rock. You've been there through the good times and not-so-good times. You've supported and encouraged me and made my dreams a reality. I love you.

To my sweet baby girl—You're the best thing that has ever happened to me. I can't imagine my life without you in it. You are my favorite girl. I love you.

9 781944 134709